The
WORK
of
CRAFT

The
WORK
of
CRAFT

*An inquiry into the nature
of crafts and craftsmanship*

With a New Introduction by the Author

Carla
Needleman

Kodansha International
New York · Tokyo · London

Kodansha America, Inc.
114 Fifth Avenue, New York, New York 10011, U.S.A.

Kodansha International Ltd.
17-14 Otowa 1-chome, Bunkyo-ku, Tokyo 112, Japan

Published in 1993 by Kodansha America, Inc.
by arrangement with Alfred A. Knopf, Inc.

*Grateful acknowledgment is made to the following for
permission to reprint previously published material:*
Grove Press, Inc.: Excerpt from Hsi K'ang on pages 105–6,
Letter to Shan T'ao, translated by H. R. Hightower,
in *Anthology of Chinese Literature,*
compiled and edited by Cyril Birch.
Copyright © 1965 by Grove Press, Inc.
Reprinted by permission.

Printed in the United States of America

93 94 95 96 6 5 4 3 2 1

Library of Congress Cataloging-in-Publication Data
Needleman, Carla
The work of craft : an inquiry into the nature of crafts and
craftsmanship / Carla Needleman.
p.   cm.
Originally published: New York : Knopf, 1979.
ISBN 4-7700-1701-4
1. Handicraft–Philosophy.   I. Title.
TT149.N43   1993   745.5'01—dc20
92-16920
CIP

Printed and bound by Arcata Graphics, Fairfield, Pennsylvania.

For my mother

Contents

Introduction

When I learned from Toinette Lippe, who edited the original edition of *The Work of Craft* for Knopf, that Kodansha International planned to reissue my book, I was pleased, but in a distant sort of way. I wrote the book fifteen years ago, after all. While it is gratifying to have my past work admired it is rather like having someone look at an old photograph and say, "You were really beautiful then"; the emotional reactions ricochet like stray bullets.

Besides, I was totally engaged at the time in finishing a book about medicine, a book in which I act as spy and double agent, sympathizing with medicine while at the same time selling its secrets to the general public. The effort to skip double-dutch back and forth over the parallel yellow lines that separate health care practitioners from the rest of us, in constant danger of being tripped up by conflicting allegiances, took all my attention.

Therefore, when Helena Franklin called on behalf of Kodansha, full of enthusiasm about *The Work of Craft*, my own enthusiasm was a bit forced. I agreed—how could I not?—to write a new introduction. But I had not read the book in years. (Authors rarely reread their own work. If it is bad one suffers, and if it is good, well, "You were beautiful *then*.")

Several months passed. The promised introduction came due. Reluctantly, very reluctantly, I sat down to read *The Work of Craft*. And—how can I say this about my former self?—she *was* beautiful then, and honest, and several other things I dare not say for fear of being thought immodest, even though she and I are no longer the same person. I owe her honorable book an honorable introduction, but I do not wish to misrepresent my present self: I no longer work at handcrafts; writing has become craft enough for me.

My recent experience as a double agent in medicine, however, may help me mediate between the makers of craft objects and the people who cherish their work. Just as doctors cannot and do not own medicine, because everyone has a body, so craftsmen do not own crafts. Craft speaks to the heart and mind through the body, our universal home, and, as this book tries to show, the work of craft is an especially fine example of the work of life, our universal obligation. Moreover, every person, although his field of practice may be abstruse, and although his experiences may seem to be specific to it, lives under that obligation and consequently in a world approachable by his fellows. We all have the same approximate shape, outside and inside, the same general categories of experience, roughly the same hopes, joys, fears, needs. The potential for understanding between people is evident, theoretically.

It is also theoretically evident that the sense of meaning and purpose in one's life, the source of personal happiness, comes through feeling a relationship not only with other people, but also with whatever higher power one recognizes, and with the world in all its variety. In practice, however, it is extraordinarily difficult to feel related. Most people feel isolated, and much of the energy expended in human life is given over to a more or less desperate (and, at the same time, fearful) search for relationship.

And yet, everything *is* related. Planets are related to other planets and to the sun; there is relationship within the atom, between molecules. Relationship on the atomic, microscopic, macroscopic, human, planetary, and universal scales may be a mystery, but it is a fact. There is exchange on all levels, a continuous call and response in obedience to the invisible force that decrees that everything be in motion and nothing exist in isolation.

People always have been driven to try to find in the universe a single, unified energy that applies equally to atoms, star systems, and human beings. It has been called gravitation, electromagnetism, God, and love. Science, religion, and art are all expressions of our hunger to understand the primary force that every person and every thing obeys.

We are unlikely to think of relationship as that primary force, however, because there seems an equal and opposite force that sets everything apart from everything else. Although we place a high value on both individuality and relationship, we experience them as contradictory. It seems we have to surrender some of our individuality (which we take to be self-determination) in order to enter into any relationship—with another person, a group, a profession, a religion, a social or political cause. We think of relationship as a transaction in which we must go out of ourselves and give over part of our substance in exchange for necessary connections with the outside world. Important as these connections are, we're afraid of giving up more than we get back, and therefore, although isolation causes us to suffer, we are under an inner compulsion to defend it. Some people, feeling that their sense of self-determination is in danger of being absorbed and effaced in the multiple entanglements of a complex world, try to keep their personal search for meaning alive through engagement in art or craft. The practice of an art or craft should serve the exploration of oneself in relationship to life. Unfortunately, art (and, less frequently, craft) can be used to support a turning aside from life.

And yet, individuality and relationship are not mutually exclusive. It is immediately apparent to the mind that only what is *not* identical can be related, that difference is intrinsic to relationship. Physical and psychic differences between forms allow the currents of dynamic tension to pass between them. Separation and relationship are two arms of the same all-encompassing embrace.

When the alchemists said *"solve et coagulo"* (which can be loosely translated as "set apart and bring together"), the transformation for which they were giving an encoded instruction was from the "lead" of human ignorance to the "gold" of realization. The chemical retort in which an individual needs to discover setting-apart-and-coming-together is himself, because the same laws that move the universe move in each one of us.

If separateness is not isolation nor relationship a negotiated bargain, individuality probably is not what we think it is either. Almost certainly it is not self-determination in our separatist sense of the word.

In order to discover for ourselves, not mentally but organically, what separateness, relationship, and individuality are, we would need to engage in an active study. Life was given us for this study, but the events of our lives carry us forward at a rapid pace. We don't know how, in the midst of the movement of life, to find how to live. If we are too cautious, try to control events, our lives feel small and cramped. At the same time, we know that circumspection does not guarantee security; life is so powerful and can be so dangerous that it is impossible to protect oneself from it. All one's careful defenses can crumble to powder in an instant. In the end, of course, old age and death know where to find us.

We need inner freedom toward life and we don't have it. Perhaps the "laboratory" of a craft can offer some experiential guidelines in how to begin to work toward transformative understanding. I must reveal that this book on craft, although far clumsier and far more limited than the writings of the alchemists, is similarly concerned more with the changes in a person than the changes worked on inert matter.

Although we would like to believe in the interrelatedness of everything existing, we find it difficult to let down our defenses sufficiently to open to the experience of it. We resist, refuse in spite of ourselves. We are neither willing nor able to give up the illusion of control. Our entirely legitimate sense that something important is at stake makes us cautious. We would prefer to look into the study before committing ourselves to it, before paying anything. We want to glimpse universal principles, if there are any, but we require validation of our separate selves also. Art and craft offer us the possibility of a foretaste of the work of life; they invite both participants and nonparticipants.

The artist spreads his sail wide to call the free wind, but his hand on the tiller guides the craft to harbor. Those of us who do not share the adventure may receive his cargo of oils and spices at no risk to ourselves. The fragrant cargo allows us to inhale the perfume of far places. If we have any taste for adventure—and it need not be for the making of art or craft objects—art encourages it in us.

In essence, art is the revelation of the universal in the specific. Great art may or may not concern itself with the mundane details of life. Craft always does. For that reason it is easier to receive. It is strange to say that an ordinary pottery mug in some small way accepts and validates the person who uses it, but it is true nonetheless. There is no intrusion; it accommodates to us, its shape and the heft of it to our hands, its lip to ours. (Even when the potter fails, when, for example, a handle shows he sacrificed function for appearance, a commonality exists; we all fail in the same ways.) Crafts pay homage to the dignity of daily life. The shape and use of the physical body is known and accepted and, in a craft object as simple as a stoneware mug, is served with modesty and love.

Using or making a piece of functional pottery can produce small moments in which, through the body, one senses a relationship with the rest of humanity. The moments are pleasant but brief. We are neither compromised nor obliged by them. They are a small gift that it is easy to accept.

On the whole, and contrary to what is commonly believed, it is much more difficult to receive than to give. People speak of wishing to give because giving makes us feel rich. Receiving makes us feel humble, grateful, and, generally speaking, most people don't like that. We experience it as a loss of control, as if we were in some way invaded or diminished by accepting a gift. The larger the gift, the more difficult it is to accept. That is why the gift of one's life, the gift of love, relationship with all of creation, or even with another person, place us in so difficult a position. I cannot bargain with or go out to the true force of relationship; either I refuse or I open to it and let it in.

Art—in every sense of the word, in every discipline both spiritual and scientific, in every aspect of life—is just this opening and letting in. It is neither self-expression nor self-determination. Sometimes it seems that nothing of real validity can get through unless all personal barriers, all opinions, all fears, all strivings, all expectations, all tensions of any kind, are out of the way. It seems a total submission is necessary. It seems impossible.

And yet—even more is required of us. Every "artist" of the art of life knows that what he is lucky enough to receive, on the rare occasions when he is available to receive it, is an active intelligence, and that the receiving itself is an active rather than a passive process. It appears to be passive only because it is not like any other action, not assertive, not insistent. But the intelligence that comes through needs to be met—that is, in me it meets itself. Energy flows into forms and is released out of them in an endless circuit. It requires our participation. It takes shape through my full and passionate acceptance of it, through my engagement with it. The personal is transformed, yes, but it isn't destroyed. Love brings strength; it doesn't make us weak. The ground of being is universal and impersonal, but it is the power out of which all manifest nature is generated. The additional requirement—not only to yield completely to the force of relationship but also to participate in it—is what makes the impossible possible. Connection with the ground of being—relationship between it and one's separate, changing self in the changing conditions of life—is the foundation of individuality and new life, the alchemists' "gold".

In order to make gold, the alchemists say, one needs to seed base metal with a little bit of gold. This book is about discovering the gleam of gold through working at a craft. One blinks and the glimmer of understanding is gone— but it can be found again. A person who wishes to become a craftsman in life, who wishes to become free to receive the force of relationship in the midst of life, will persist. Alchemy is not alone in offering the possibility of trans- formation. All traditions speak of it, calling it by different names. All say, also, that it requires a long preparatory study. The work of craft is a preparation, one of many.

October 1992,
San Francisco

The
WORK
of
CRAFT

Pottery: A Personal Exploration

The need for positive results is so much a part of our way of life, the attitude of the achiever is so fixed in us, that we scarcely can envision a different way of life. We stand in so peculiar a relationship to results that the products of our own hands bring about a confusion in us. We need to know, right away, whether they are good or bad; we need to know, to pin down, to decide, so that we will know how to feel. The fact of our lives is uncertainty, and we crave certainty. The fact of our lives is change, movement, and we long for "arriving."

I don't know what to feel when I look at a pot I've made. The relationship between myself and this object, my production which now exists independently of me, is ambiguous and unsure. There is something I need to understand that I don't know how to ask about, a question that can't form itself in me past the first word: why? Or perhaps: how? There must be a right question if only I knew how to frame it. Where to begin?

I have, I realize, already begun. My medium is, accidentally or by natural inclination, pottery. I will need to be very sensitive, to attend very carefully to my movement in the studio if I am to look for the unknown in the only place it can be real to me, here in the midst of the known.

What is it to make something? I knew this clay before it was born, when it was nothing, just a special kind of dirt. I wedged it so that it became even and smooth, without air bubbles, a consistent something and not just a chunk torn off a bigger chunk. I put it on the wheel and put the wheel in motion and with a steady pressure of my hands brought the clay into roundness. My fingers made a well in the center of the roundness and my left hand went inside and pulled over toward my right hand to make the base. The two hands together squeezed the clay and pulled it up into a cylinder, a simple form.

Then I tried to understand something about form through the medium of this very flexible material. The locked-in pattern of my habitual thought quickly came in to fill the space beginning to open in me. I became aware of a moment of tension as the thought tried to answer, to protect me from the helplessness of not knowing.

I wondered again why I bother, what there is about pottery that draws me again and again to this moment of unsureness. Why do I keep coming back, keep making mediocre pots? The clay passed through several transitory shapes on the theme of a single curve. What in me monitors the shapes, rejecting some and accepting others? I experienced a kind of impatience, a wish to choose. Finally I liked the shape. It was apparent that the choice was a victory of the need to choose, to settle on something, over the need to experience something new.

I went on. The shoulder, neck, and lip of the pot had to

be brought into correspondence with the body. I took the easy way out; I "did" it, "made" them, feeling only slightly uneasy. Thought told me that I didn't have *time* to wait for exactly the right lip to appear to me. I tasted what it is in me that meets the world; I have made this shape before. I took the pot off the wheel and set it aside. The next day, when it was firm enough, I trimmed away the excess clay. I trimmed too much, some of the vitality of the pot was sacrificed to a superficial sophistication of form. It is very familiar. The pot was put to dry. Weeks later it was fired. The fired pot was "pleasant," I told myself.

I painted a design on it. It took me hours and I worked with a great deal of care and concentration. Nevertheless, what I call "impatience," the need to get on with it, kept the design ordinary. I glazed the pot and fired it again. When I first saw it, in the first moment when I took it out of the kiln and the pot was new to me, I realized that the lip is weak, that the curve is far from subtle. The pot is very light. I remembered briefly that the lightness is more from the trimming than the throwing, but it doesn't show and I put the thought aside. In all honesty, and the moment of honesty is terribly short, I don't know how I feel about this pot.

The discomfort of this moment is very like the discomfort of searching for form on the wheel. I sense that in the need to decide whether I'm pleased or displeased with the pot, pleased or displeased with the way I worked at making it, pleased or displeased with myself as a potter, as a person, in this either/or I close myself off from the living wholeness of experience. But the moment passes and I decide—it's a decent pot with some not too obvious flaws.

5

For me this is what it's like to work at a craft. This is what *really* takes place.

I am not suggesting that the attitude toward results is the only attitude conditioning the way a craftsman works or even that this attitude can be, or is, obvious to me every time I sit down at the wheel. To suggest that would be to hang everything on one hook, an unwise procedure no matter how big the hook is. I do suggest that the desire to succeed is the progenitor of real failure and that this attitude is a far more subtly pervasive force than we realize. We don't recognize it because our lives do not offer us other options. The craving for results in objects, or in opinions, the need to name, the need to "know," which means to end the discomfort of not knowing, is the seemingly innocuous backdrop against which all our activities take place. I don't know how to feel about the pot because I don't know how to feel about myself. The pot and I then make a closed circle in which no new knowledge can enter precisely because it hasn't been asked for.

I enter the studio on a sunny morning. I've slept well and had a satisfying breakfast. My body feels fit and relaxed and I look forward to working. I take some clay out of the bin and carry it to the wedging table. The clay smells musty and good. I notice that my thumbs move on the surface of the clay, testing the texture of it and taking pleasure in the sensation. I begin to wedge, rotating the clay upon itself. My left foot is forward, right foot back, and I rock between them, exaggerating the movement a little, enjoying how it coordinates with my breathing. The left hand supports the clay, the right pushes, so that little by little the clay rocks, I rock, and the wheel of the clay turns, making a shape like a conch, very beautiful.

The exercise of wedging makes me feel warm; the air in the room had felt chilly when I started. I cut the clay on a wire fixed across the table and throw one of the pieces on the table, cut side away from me, trying to get the right sound—a loud thwack that means the clay has hit all at the same time. I reverse the other piece so that the cut edges will be opposite each other and throw it on the first with the full force of the natural downswing of my arms. I rock the clay to release it from the table and cut it again. The wire vibrates and hums. The clay slams on the table— thwack, thwack. I am part of a rhythm of sound and move- ment and I keep it up a few more times for the pleasure of it. I form the clay into three balls and take it to the wheel, the kick wheel this morning, not the electric wheel.

I fix a plaster batt to the wheelhead and gather my tools: a bowl of water and a sponge, a needle, a rib, a strip of chamois, and a broken plaster batt for the wet clay slurry that comes off on my hands when I work. I push the wheel slightly with my right foot and drop the clay onto the cen- ter of the wheel. I pat the clay with the palms of both hands as the clay turns, slapping it into a good position for the work of centering. I place my left foot on the support on the side of the wheel and lay my hands on my lap relaxed. I turn the left hand palm up to remind myself to *stay* relaxed. My back is straight. I'm ready to begin kick- ing the wheel.

The kick comes from the knee, the foot engaging the flywheel close to the edge and following around until the leg is extended. I allow the lower leg to return to its flexed position, to rest on the way back, and kick again. I use the momentum of the wheel to increase the momentum, kicking again and again, not tiring myself, aware of the sensation of the kicking leg, of the sensation of the relaxed left leg, trying to kick better each time with the least expenditure of energy. When the wheel is going quite fast I stop kicking, place my foot on the support to the right, and wet my hands. The two hands squeeze the clay at the base of the mound, forcing it up. The palms then push on the top of the clay, pushing it down again. My hands are steady, not riding the irregularities of the clay mound, but mastering the clay with steady pressure.

Much has been said about centering but it has little to do with the actual work of centering. The clay will come on center in response to a simple line of force from any direction. I can squeeze the clay, push down on it, push away from myself, pull toward myself—the clay on the rapidly spinning wheel will come on center. When the wheel slows I kick it up again, never allowing it to lose its momentum. Centering can easily be done with the eyes closed. I close my eyes now and sense the clay riding true between my hands. I have a deep sense of well-being, a kind of joyful seriousness, a potentiality.

The three procedures described, wedging, kicking, and centering, each undertaken strictly for its own sake, without direct reference to what is to follow, prepare the potter as much as they do the clay. It is a ritual, much like the long preparatory grinding of the ink stick in sumi painting, feet flat on the floor if sitting at a table, left palm flat on the table, to quiet the mind and bring the relaxed thought to attend to the sensations of the body. Feeling as we ordinarily know it, the "I like, I don't like; I want, I don't want" sort of feelings, practically vanish or, when they appear, fail to attract the interest of the mind, engaged as it is in something so much more interesting to it. The purer, more subtle attention becomes aware of more subtle feeling. It is here that the process often is brought to a halt. The feeling, something like wonder, is so new that the avaricious mind arouses and turns fully toward it, to grasp it, abandoning in that sudden turning the integrative process of study that had made the moment possible. Thought, so much slower than feeling, enters in and, finding something precious no longer there, attempts to reconstruct in words so as to salvage the experience by remembering it. Many intellectually stimulating ideas about craftsmanship, full of interesting connections, have their genesis in such a moment. But, looking back upon such verbal constructions of my own, I find that not one of them ever helped me to become a better craftsman.

The realization that when I work at my craft in a way that allows each moment to fall of its own weight, without hurrying it or retaining it, such a way of working will produce in me a state of greater sensitivity, can lead me to use this method as an inner technique having as its goal the state itself, solely for the pleasure of it. It is undeniably a great pleasure. When my hands, working together in perfect unison, move slowly up the side of an emerging pot, raising the walls higher and higher, and I see the marks of my fingers on the sides clearly and evenly spaced, I am happy. Then there is no other place I would like to be, no other activity I would prefer to engage in. If I use the craft for the sake of its pleasures, its sensations, even if by that I mean the sensation of inner peace, I am using it as therapy. It is true that I am in need of therapy. I need to quiet my tumbled thoughts and feelings and relax a body otherwise tensed against all the impingements of the outer and inner worlds. I am grateful that the craft has the capacity to heal me. But if I am content to be content, it is the most the craft will be able to give me. I will have given up the possibility of learning, and I will have done so for pleasure's sake, no matter how rarefied and exceptional the pleasure is.

Besides, and I suppose fortunately, it doesn't always happen that the day and I are sunny. There are times when the clay is too hard or too soft, wedging tires me, there's a draft from somewhere on my feet, and I seem to have forgotten how to throw. I overestimate the strength of the clay and the pot collapses. The next ball of clay unaccountably refuses to stick to the wheelhead. At last it does. I raise it into a cylinder and begin to shape it only to find a piece of sponge in the wall. I dig out the sponge and try to patch the hole—to no avail. Beginning with another ball of clay, I find that I'm using too much water, an indication to me that I'm not in control of the clay. I rush to center it, feeling how much time I've wasted, and have trouble. I don't like the sound of the bearing on the wheel and there seems to be a wobble at high speeds. I begin to make the opening before the clay is properly centered and when I pull it up the top is uneven. I cut it with the needle and when I pull it up again find I have to cut still more off the top. There is more clay discarded on the table than there is on the wheel. I try to breathe evenly and slow down, to imitate the precise movements of the days when everything goes right, but it's just an external imitation, no use, an obvious pretense. I'm aggressive, I attack the clay, can't do anything right, get tired, dirty, and miserable, produce two pots I know then and there I'm going to break up tomorrow, and stop for the day. Some therapy.

It is difficult to know what attitude of mind to have toward such days. The temptation is to dismiss them. If I didn't work as a craftsman, why admit that event into a study of craftsmanship? Why not deal only with the "better" days? But some habit of economy prevents me from taking this road. What a pity it would be to discard whole days as if they had never happened when even the trimmings from a pot are saved and reused. And, more important, if I am looking in the craft for something truly unknown I need to be very careful not to abandon prematurely an area of possible research. On what grounds would I leave out these times? I may say they are beside the point, they don't occur very often, they are basically not interesting, but the real reason is, I don't want to include them because they are embarrassing. Now that's the truth. And if I am searching for truth as I claim, isn't the truth of my incompetence and how I react to it just as valuable as the truth about competence?

Let us look more carefully at these days of useless struggle and embarrassing incompetence. When I face them without turning away, what is the direct result? It is obvious, right away, that if I include these days in my history, I cannot tell myself too many comforting lies about being a craftsman. A day such as I've described puts me back at the beginning, shows me how little I know, and, by returning me from my self-importance, sets me again in my own skin, smaller, and more human.

Sometimes, more frequently than I even now wish to acknowledge, I approach my craft with the full panoply of civilized "virtues"—arrogance, self-pity, cunning, irritation, laziness, impatience. To be sure, I share these features and the manifestations of them with the world at large, these "blessings" do not define me alone. This does not blunt the edge of the realization that these things live in me, but it may make it easier to bear. What a range there is in human life, from the narrowest distrust of experience to the most open and intelligent awareness. These few descriptions I've given—how different from one another they are. What is the craft of being human? The material, myself, that I have to work with constantly changes. It has qualities of clay, glass, metal, wood, wool; it is brittle, flexible, malleable, obdurate. It is as if the study of being human is the ultimate craft and all the crafts reflections of it.

If the study of myself is my real purpose in working at a craft, how will that affect my approach to the craft? (I must remember, right at the outset, that by formulating a statement of intention, I make it easier for myself to ignore it completely. We keep conclusions on our mental shelves, like trophies, and show them off to visitors, but they don't really enter into our lives.) What does it mean that I undertake to study *myself*? It seems patently ridiculous to partition myself along yet another artificial line of division; I am already fragmented enough. Perhaps it can mean instead that I extend myself into the craft, willing to sacrifice any of my opinions that experience proves false. I undertake to begin a conversation with the craft, to listen to it, to be taught by the effort of trying to understand it. Perhaps through the exchange a richer way of experiencing will begin to take root in me. I can be fairly sure that "myself" is not what I think it is—hardly anything, on close examination, proves to be what I thought. So, for selfish reasons I undertake a selfless study. It is sufficiently illogical to bring about the sensation of a newness in me.

The shift in emphasis from the craft to the craftsman takes place in the mind first. I began by being attracted to a craft, to pottery, although it might perhaps have been some other craft, and by working at the craft over a long period of time I became aware of *how* I work at it. I started out with a vision, an idealized picture of the craftsman at work. I visualized myself becoming more and more proficient, learning from my mistakes and producing increasingly more beautiful pots. I imagined that I could be dedicated and serious and saw myself as if from outside, sitting at the wheel in a large, orderly studio filled with pottery in various stages of completion, my head bent in concentration, all my movements sure and purposeful. The vision never completely faded. When I speak to people about what I do and what pottery is for me I still sometimes speak from this vision. But over the years some of the luster has faded from the picture. The beautiful dream began to be less satisfying, disrupted by the less than beautiful truth. When I spoke of pottery in idealistic terms, of myself as a Potter, I began to hear little voices telling me it wasn't quite true, and I was ashamed. I had begun to realize that the obstacles to living the vision were in myself and that they were not a matter of technique.

It became increasingly clear that I work at pottery exactly the way I do everything else and that what was wrong with the vision was that I had left myself out, my habits, my feelings, my way of living in the world. When I saw that I made the same few forms in pottery again and again, I tried to change the form by working harder at shaping the pot. Gradually I became aware that the pot was a reflection of my inadequate and false self-image. If, for example, I see myself as a direct and forthright person I will make sturdy pots with simple straight sides, what passes for "honest" pottery; if I see myself as graceful the pots will reflect this image. But always there is something missing, something not quite right, out of touch, because the self-image is a partial, deluded one, a persona instead of the expression of a person, instead of a true individuality. There are real differences between people and real limits, but they are masked, not only from others (who often see through the pretense) but especially from ourselves. It doesn't help to try to produce a different shape on the wheel. I've tried. The "new" form was a bad imitation of an invented image, not a new form at all but only a sham opposite to the persona. It didn't seem that there was a way out. It became necessary to go back to the vision, to examine it. Could it be that it too was merely an idealization, a projection of a falsehood, just another daydream?

And if it was, what was left for me? I had been forced by experience to the knowledge that I didn't know how to become a craftsman. The more I tried to force it, the more tension there was. By resisting a thing we evoke it and reinforce its existence, nourish it, keep it alive—the more I resisted the powerful forces preventing open communication with the clay, the more fixed they became in me. Through all this time an unnoticed process had been taking place. I had begun to see small but undeniable truths about myself, and had begun to be interested in seeing them. The emphasis was shifting. A new attitude was forming, and attitude is everything. I had come to realize that the solidly entrenched attitude toward results, "success," poisoned all my efforts and that *I could not change it.* I wanted to make beautiful pottery and that desire, a kind of avarice, prevented me. As I began to be more and more interested in what the craft was revealing to me of myself, I became interested in this attitude. That is, I began to take the attitude itself as material, just as the clay is material.

A craft is, can be, an education in failure, an education in the attitude toward failure, an education in and transformation of my attitude toward failure. I have been wanting to speak of this since I began to write. Each time it occurred as a word in my thoughts, "failure" carried with it that sinking sensation so intimately associated with it in all our ordinary life. It carried with it the finality, the absence of movement characteristic of dead things, to which the automatic human reaction is helpless discouragement. But I can't find another or better word to speak of this most important approach to the lesson of crafts. I fail and I go on. Failure is a beginning, failure is the springboard of hope. The more I can bear to risk to fail, the more, like Antaeus, contact with the earth will renew my life. This needs some explanation.

We have been speaking throughout this chapter of the

need for success as being a constrictive force that bars me from immediate participation in the moment as it appears, prevents the all-important conversation with the material of the craft, prevents openness of relationship, prevents a kind of quickness of response much swifter than the cautions of the mind. The need for success distorts pleasure, rendering acceptable only "materialism," the "gimme" approach to everything from a well-made piece of work to a new feeling or sensation. Pleasure becomes materialistic when it rests on the storing up of goods, a material concept whether the goods themselves are material or not.

The need for success and the fear of failure are two aspects of the same inner attitude. For it isn't failure that causes the sinking sensation we all know, but the fear of failure. Failure isn't the enemy—fear is. One learns, after all, by failing. This is elementary; we all know it, except when it applies to ourselves at the moment when I fail.

How can a craft teach us to be?

A friend asked me to make some plates for him. I had made a few plates before but I'd never made a project out of it, never studied plates. I discovered very quickly that plates were more difficult than I had thought. My first plates were too flat. I didn't really know what plates look like! I went to the kitchen for a bit of research. A plate is really a very shallow bowl. Back to the wheel. The next plates had a lift at the edge but there was something intangibly wrong with all of them. I wanted a continuous curve from edge to edge and I couldn't get it right, something happened just at the place where the lift began. I knew there was a move—some way of holding the hands —and I couldn't find it. I wanted the plates thin, the curve exact, the surface smooth. Each plate was a failure, and each failure drew my interest more and more. I became less interested in making plates and more interested in studying how the learning process proceeds in me. After a while, in a week or so, I could fake a plate. That is, the end product looked like a smooth perfect plate—but it didn't look "happy." No wonder; it took me at least twenty minutes to torture the lump of clay into the shape I wanted, smoothing it with a rib, going back over the curve again and again to get it right; all of this confusion and laboriousness showing in the finished product, at least to my eye. I would not accept these plates as a success. I insisted on my right to take them as failures because I wanted to go on. Success is a destination; one gets off the train and has to find something else to do. I was too interested to stop yet.

There came a day when my hands found how to move and I produced my first real plate. The people who had been following my plate adventure (I tend to talk a lot about what interests me) saw as I did—this one was a plate and the others, the ones that looked like plates, were a pretense. I produced a few more and stopped for the day. The next time I came to the studio I came to "make" plates, and of course my hands had forgotten how. I had given up the joy of study, the Way of failure, and had fallen again into the dead end of success.

There is more to the plate story. I could go on about the study of trimming the bottom of the plate to get the foot rim, the various discoveries I made about how dry the plate has to be before it can be trimmed, where to place the rim so that the plate looks right on a table, how to tap the bottom of the plate with a finger while trimming and listen to the sound to know how thin the bottom is getting. I could speak of how to allow the plates to dry slowly to avoid warping. The effort to find the right glaze is part of it too, a big part. All the time in producing dinnerware one has to think of people using it—colors that appeal to the appetite, the sound a utensil will make on this particular glaze. But the effort of precision, the search for perfection, is not undertaken for the sake of the finished product. If I don't have a goal, an aim, how will I know when I fall short? But if I have only the goal how will I see where I am now? It is failure (with its emotional impact included) that can recall me to myself, bridging the gap between vision and action, making of all a field for study.

Just what *is* study? I have spoken of study within a craft and even of the craftsman's study of himself through a craft. But it seems to me that all these years I have been learning *how* to study, never quite sure of my direction, getting lost and finding my way again, engaged in a nameless and rather private struggle to understand.

What is study? What is the attitude of a student? How is the craftsman, in the way in which he approaches his craft after twenty years as well as when he first begins, a student? And is it really true that when he, at moments or forever, ceases to be a student he just then stops being a craftsman? Surely when I first began I knew nothing about pottery and I wanted to learn; I could not help being a student in the most obvious sense of the word. Surely now, after all this time, I know something about the craft, even quite a bit; I cannot still be a student in the same way. And yet I feel that the attitude of a student is the first and last principle of craftsmanship and that without it work at a craft is superficial and banal.

When I began to learn pottery I knew nothing about it as a craft. I came to it, therefore, with a natural attitude of not knowing and it was possible, with interest and persistence, to learn. I did not have to work for that attitude; it is, so to speak, written into the beginnings of things. After a time, when the technique of the craft had become more or less habitual to my body, knowing replaced not knowing and the mind, always lazy, always seeking self-satisfaction, rested there. We are all like this, I think; what we do moderately well we enjoy doing again and again for the pleasure of the skill, for the pleasure of competence. I have a territory and am unwilling to give it up, to forsake "knowing" for the unknown with all its uncertainty. "Knowing" is riches and I am unwilling to be poor.

The sensation of emptiness, of poverty in the feelings, is associated with the sensation of emptiness in the body when my stomach is empty. Instead of valuing it—it is possibility—I wish, as quickly as I can, to fill up, not to be empty any more. For me, as for most of us, the finer sensations of the feelings are too readily confused with the accustomed sensations of the body, habits acquired even in infancy dictating to an unaware adult how to feel.

This same unaware adult, me, invents theories, spins a philosophy, all because the child that runs my life believes and has convinced the rest of me that all emptiness is a form of physical hunger, a signal from the organism to fill up, to make the sensation go away.

Is there anywhere in the loosely associated parts that

make up what I call Myself, a federalizing force, a grown-up? Is there anything firm enough to resist the impulse to gratify all desires immediately? Anything wise enough to put up with some discomfort for the sake of a greater good? In plain words, what can help me bear the awful feeling of uncertainty? The further I go with my craft, the bigger it gets, the less understandable it becomes, the fewer ordinary satisfactions it gives me, the less fun it is, until I begin to ask—why am I doing this? This isn't what I started for—I just wanted to enjoy making pottery. I'd better just forget the whole thing, give it up.

At this point the craftsman in whatever craft has come to a crossroad. He can indeed give up the pursuit of the unattainable, the mastery of a craft through the ordinary means of greater technical skill. He can, as many do, switch to a different craft, going "on" to weaving or glass-blowing, even at this point pretending to himself that he wishes the challenge of learning again, when actually what he wants is the gratification of the rapid learning process at the beginning of a craft. At the beginning it is simple ignorance that stands in my way—later on it is "knowing" that blocks me.

But suppose the craftsman is drawn despite discomfort to continue, suppose he has glimpsed the god in his craft, the magic of the possibility of a new way of living the craft. Even then he is in danger—because this new understanding is not permanent. At any moment he, I, can choose the cynicism of the known and go on making what I well know how to make, not extending myself into the line of the unknown. Or I can become a hypocrite—play it safe and lie about my so-called serious explorations. I can branch aside within the craft and study, for example, glaze chemistry, a reasonable, necessary, unarguably practical pursuit, but one that can be as much a turning aside from the question of my craft as if I had discarded the craft for another.

The question of my craft is the question of myself—Who am I?—a question the craft can help me to rediscover again and again and yet again at just those moments at which I experience that I don't know. The experience of myself in question is for me a moment of a different level of certainty. It is an experience, not a thought—it does not have to be in words—and there is with it not a shred of self-pity or of pride or of so-called humility—it is so, undeniably true, neither good nor bad, but real. I cannot bring myself into question by deciding that it is a good thing and trying it. But I find that if I try to work honestly at a craft, not turning away when the going gets rough, these moments of myself in question will come. And if the experience occurs often enough, it acts to transform my understanding, chemically and from within.

I experience a kind of uneasiness when I hear people speak about "being centered." The expression is taken from pottery, from the clay being brought into harmony on the rapidly spinning wheel so that it appears not to move in the midst of movement. The expression, translated into the human, personal sphere, means quiet and balance, harmony in the midst of the turmoil of life. It is difficult to argue with what seems to be a state that it is natural for any normal person to wish for. Yet there has always been that nagging doubt in me, an irritation that I've been at a loss to account for. When the clay is centered, it is possible to begin. But those who speak, so facilely, of "being centered" take it as an end. It may be the point at which I am able to be in question as, with clay, it is the point at which the question of form, the question of purpose, can begin. A balanced lump is still a lump and to stop there, to admire it, is to me a sinful shirking of responsibility. The clay before it is put on the wheel is "innocent"—it has not yet been touched by intention. But once the force of intention has been brought to bear upon it, once it has been put on the wheel and, through being centered, has acquired a preliminary integrity, the same laws that applied to it when it was just a hunk of special dirt no longer apply. When I simply live my life as it comes to me, as a child does, I am innocent. But once I begin to have a direction, to discover who I am and what my purpose is, I come under a different set of laws, of conditions, which, taken in the aggregate, do not intend or care about my comfort. When people speak of "being centered" I often suspect that what they mean is that they "feel" centered, they feel good. It seems to be a degradation of a state that can have a real meaning and I react to hearing it as if it were a kind of blasphemy, which it may well be.

The laws of craft and the teachings of any particular real craft run parallel to the craft of being human. The mind, however, thinks of analogy as a kind of game it plays, as an invention of the mind through which thought delights in its own limberness. The mind treats the mentally accessible analogies between craft and one's life as if they existed solely as the product of and for the indulgence of mental gymnastics. It simply doesn't take analogy seriously.

But to apply what I see in crafts too glibly to what I see of my life does not take into account that I see very little of my life. It cheapens the teaching of a craft by diminishing it and cuts me off from the possibility of learning. The craft, moreover, does not apply to ordinary life but to the extraordinary—the life of study. The pot, for example, goes through the fire and is transformed. *I do not know what this means. There is no parallel in my life.* It may be that there *can* be. But I will not learn about fire by thinking about fire but by burning.

Speculative imagination is useless. If it were possible to learn through speculative analogy, the craft would not be necessary. The craft teaches precisely through bypassing the self-indulgent speculative part of the mind that would rather think about working than work. The craft provides experience. I can learn through the order of experiences contained in a craft if I am willing not to be hasty in drawing conclusions and if I am willing not to think I know better and can manipulate the order of experiences. The craft will lead me if I am able to put aside my impatience and follow.

If clay is Adam and if I am that clay before creation, before Adam, I must not decide beforehand what I'd like to be. Otherwise I will lead with my mind, and the mind, in the life study of a craft, needs to be passive, to be there but to be passive, to watch without putting an end to a process by summing up. If the part that should be passive takes an active role in creation, I will create not Man but monkey, a monstrous distortion.

The craft is an analogy, a living symbol, of Man. If I wish to live fully I need to put aside my one-leveled, exclusively mental logic and live *ana*logically, or at least try to. The life of analogy is the life of levels of meaning. Explanation, on the other hand, is the attempt to coalesce levels. Explanation of symbol is the attempt to capture on one level the reciprocal exchange of energies between levels. And so, for most of us, symbol hardly exists. We live in our heads and symbol cannot be comprehended by the isolated intellect.

When I look at pottery from, say, the Islamic world, or at even fairly recent American Indian pottery, I am so touched by it. It is so real, so beautiful and so unaffected, so mysteriously good, and I don't understand how they were able to produce such pottery when I—with access to far better clay, kilns far easier to fire, and the electric wheel for goodness' sake!—just blunder along. I mention this here because it seems to have bearing on the whole question of what a life of meaning is.

The great craft works have come to us out of traditional societies. I find it now very difficult to think of what a traditional society is and how it came to be. I hold at the same time two contradictory feelings about these societies, the one an emotional longing for a life of order and the other a kind of irritation when I try to picture myself within such a society; it seems so restrictive of what we have all learned to call personal freedom.

Yet I am not free to enjoy my freedom. Even in my craft, as I have seen, I am not free to make any shape I wish. The shapes I make are determined by the various forms of my self-image, and the "choices" of self-image, if I may use such a word as "choice," are predetermined by the influences, pressures, education, world outlook, of the society I live in. I am constrained by the existential space in which I live. An almost simplistic definition of "society" is that it is a space, a living space: a society *is* the emotional climate, the acceptable ideas, desires, ways of life, of the people in it. When I find it emotionally unpalatable to be limited, as it seems traditional potters often were, to a very few traditional shapes, is it really that the need for so-called free choice originates in me or is that need conditioned in me by this society? Because if it is the latter it isn't the love of freedom that speaks in me but rather the love of slavery, familiar slavery.

I am not a production potter. I don't make great numbers of a single form as quickly as possible in order to sell them. I don't supply my own household with all its dinnerware and other ceramic containers. I sell a few things, give some away, keep a few. My craft is not, in any practical sense, a necessity. This places me in the unfortunate limbo of "art." There is a common misconception that craft slides into art when the object made is no longer useful for anything. The things I make are useful, but if I don't use them, don't need to use them, does that rob what I do of meaning? Am I just a hobbyist justifying what I do by long speeches that make it sound important—something like an elderly lady feeding pigeons in the park? Does meaning derive from usefulness? This isn't rhetoric, please bear with me. I need to feel that my life serves some purpose and is not just an interval between birth and death. I don't know why I'm here and, as a matter of fact, I hardly know *that* I am here. Doesn't everyone, a doctor, a secretary, a mother, have these moments of terrible doubt —what is it all for? And, because these doubts are un-answerable, and because they make us unhappy, we, as relatively sane people, turn aside from futile questions, turn aside and continue with whatever it is we do.

Our whole society is predicated on the assumption that since real meaning is undiscoverable, is either the province of an unreachable but presumably merciful God or is in fact nonexistent, we would do best to keep busy, keep mov-ing, and not think about it, finding as much as we can of admittedly transitory happiness. There are in our society those who claim to give us answers—religions and pseudo-religions, most of them devotional in nature, asking "only" for faith and offering us tranquillity in exchange for the sacrifice of our questions. For the most part they appeal to our emotional side and seem to leave a great deal out of consideration—they seem to have no recognition of how very complicated life is. Many young people, particularly in these times, find this kind of answer almost hypnotically attractive.

There is the answer of science—to further the advance-ment of human knowledge; it substitutes different ques-tions for questions of meaning, taking up the "space for questioning" with questions that relate to measurement, quantity, and various forms of analysis and new synthesis (theory) on the level of analysis. Science redefines what questions are askable by calling a question only one that can have a rational answer by men such as ourselves.

The ethical professions in their most pure manifestations, dedicated doctors, psychiatrists, concerned teachers, some members of all the helping professions and even some legislators, some clergy, all those whose aim and work in life is to relieve suffering—what of them? They do so much good, we all, if we stop to think about it, have been given cause several times in our lives to be grateful to them. Surely our search for a life of meaning, a purposeful existence, can look here for its resolution in a life of service. But the very best of these good people are most seriously in doubt. Suffering is endlessly regenerated, a many-headed hydra, and good men cannot agree among themselves about what help for man consists of. Direct action on manifest suffering alone isn't enough. An understanding is missing, a core of meaning has been lost.

Having dismissed in short order most religion, science, and service to humanity as in one way or another failing to meet us at the level of our deepest questioning, where shall we turn? To art? The practice of art seems to encourage in almost all artists a kind of introspection that even to the most casually inquiring eye leads in the opposite direction entirely from real questioning. Else why would they be so vain, so "interestingly" unbalanced? So easily hurt by criticism, so susceptible to flattery? Evidently the character of artists is "deliberately," as it were, formed on the basic misunderstanding that real discovery can be made by intensifying one area of sensitivity at the expense of others. It causes an increasing pathology, as if one were to train oneself in so-called psychic powers while neglecting totally to try to understand the foundation from which such special talents come. The artist looks introspectively within himself—that is, he takes himself *as he is* as a source of meaning—he believes what he sees there. He expresses with paint, clay, metal, film, the inner muddle which is our common lot, and is taken as a "bad," "good," or "great" artist depending on the degree of success he has in expressing this muddle. But he doesn't see it as what it is, as muddle and nothing more, but as expressive of Truth, Reality, Beauty, or something else with a capital letter. The craftsmen are mostly caught in the same trap as the artists, except that their ambition and hence their pathology is somewhat less; lowercase cousins of the Artists.

But I object, no less I'm sure than anyone else, to my seemingly offhand dismissal of art. Art, science, religion, humanitarianism, are the main human endeavors and as such *have* to be the sources of a life of meaning. Why then do we fail to find what we need in them? If the causes for the thwarted hunger in us for meaning cannot be found in the areas of human endeavor themselves, then we must look to ourselves, to how we have failed to come to them properly. Because clearly in other times and in other cultures, science, art, music, medicine, religion, were the great vehicles of integrative study. One has only to spend an hour or two at a museum looking at antiquities to feel the *wisdom* of ancient peoples, to feel the power of their creative thrust, and to feel, if I am not lost in false rapture, that by comparison I am impotent by reason of my ignorance. It is harder to look with unclouded eyes at science, medicine. We have been conditioned to regard alchemy as superstition, the forerunner, merely, of modern chemistry, and at various traditional systems of medicine as the heroic efforts of people before the time of the germ theory to effect cures on the basis of inadequate information. We are very free with the word "superstition." As a sad and funny example: When skeletons of a long-vanished tribe were found with pieces of skull cut out, it was explained by saying that these primitive people had no doubt removed the pieces of bone from their bravest fallen warriors in order to wear them as protective amulets. It was only recently that someone noticed that in the skulls they found, there was evidence of regeneration of bone around the edges of the cut—therefore the surgery had been done on the living, not the dead, trepanning to relieve pressure on the brain after a severe head wound, and the patient had survived. Is our quickness to label some practices of ancient or "primitive" cultures "superstition" a kind of protective verbal amulet we wear?

Our own culture is not in very good shape. There is too much poverty, too much crime, too much just plain unhappiness around us. We are polluting the air and the oceans, denuding the forests, killing off whole species of animals. We fight wars on a previously unimaginably vast scale. Our foods are more and more prepared with chemical additives or through chemical processes. Cancer and heart disease are on the increase. And so on and so forth. Obviously we are doing something wrong. And, just as obviously, we aren't able to stop. The attempt to solve the problems of modern life all too often just overlays a new source of misery on top of the one it was calculated to solve.

We can't go back, back to an agrarian society, crafts, guilds, the ceremonies of the American Indians, back to any of the forms of life that draw us through our discontent and our sentimentality. We are ourselves living in the twentieth century. We want something, need something, and when we look at vanished cultures, we sometimes imagine that we understand what it is they had that is missing in our lives. I doubt it. What we see, we see with modern eyes, and what we see are the various *results* of a more authentic approach to life, not the approach, not the attitude itself. Our senses, our understanding, have become too gross, we are magnetized to results, attracted or repelled by them. We do not *see* means. If we did we wouldn't be in the mess we are now. We would be able to predict results on the basis of an understanding of the means we use, and not be so surprised all the time at how badly things have turned out when we meant so well.

Action is all the time swallowing us alive, swallowing up our life. But, hidden to us, every movement is both action and reaction as, in the human body, each movement, even the smallest shift of a finger, involves a set of muscles, adductor and extensor, one that contracts and one that allows the contraction. The dual nature of action is easily forgotten in every field of life. *Homo faber*, man the maker, appears to have forgotten that all work is half rest. There is a movement and a return, whether in swinging an ax, walking, kicking a potter's wheel, thinking, or feeling. Without *both*, action is frantic and misguided, movement is tense and unrhythmical, the feelings are excessive, and thought climbs from conclusion to conclusion building its tower on sand. The common purpose, the relationship between people, the link within a community, has its genesis in this great law of breath, going out and coming in. It is the craft, the skillful means, of life. But when I am committed so totally and to the exclusion of everything else to action and result, to doing, making, building, nothing is connected. I fight myself, grow angry, desperate, even cynical—there seems to be no hope, no meaning. We need to learn not what to do, we need to learn to allow the law of breath to be immanent in our lives.

An idea is not a set of words, a handle to make it easier for me to grasp things. It isn't something outside myself, a tool that I use; it is alive, not metaphorically but actually alive. If I try to use it in the way that I use everything else, I make it into a dead thing and it cannot help me. Every living thing, even a plant that I accept into my home, is capable of the unexpected. It has its own integrity in which it needs to be respected. (That I do not respect it shows my lack of reverence for life—in a plant, in a person, in an idea, even in myself for the life within me that moves me.) An idea can help me only if I accept it into myself and give it room. I need to watch and not be hasty. Some plants require direct sunlight, some do best in diffused light, some need to be kept moist, some to dry out. What conditions are necessary for ideas to flourish? Some need thinking about and some germinate best in silence. Some need to be acted upon frequently and some, if they are made to be active in my life before they are fully rooted in me, will shrivel and die. Opinions are a different matter; they spring up like weeds in any unguarded soil. But a living idea is a force for good.

If I try to "do" an idea I take it on my own old terms and not within the space of the idea itself. Then I don't give it room and it will suffocate, leaving behind only its shell, only the words.

Am I supposed to do nothing? All of this is more than confusing; it's confounding. Our search for meaning seems to have led us to a standstill. Or has it? Am I not still trying to solve the problem, trying to understand it, pin it down, am I not impatient, tapping my feet with the impatience of wanting to get on with it, wondering how on earth this lengthy philosophical dead end is going to lead back to the question of crafts? I don't stand still. I *can't* stand still. I even make a virtue out of restlessness, calling it the energy of life, or some such foolish phrase. The best definition of hellfire I ever heard called hellfire just that, starting a movement and not being able to stop it. What does it take to stop me? I begin to recognize the magnitude of the problem.

I am all the time overshooting the mark. When I go out, I go too far. When I am making a circular pot, I think of completing the circle while my hands are working on the base. I'm always pointing at things and getting lost in the things, not staying with the finger pointing. When I see a person I could simply take in that impression, but I begin to think about the person and so on. I am never where I am. It is a shock to realize this. I need to let that shock in, to allow it really to shock me. And then, when I let the shock in, there is a sense of danger. The sense of danger bolts me to my spot. I feel myself in danger because what I am in essence is threatened. My essential meaning is threatened. And here, in danger, I return to myself. A moving equilibrium, my "breath" returns to me and circulates within the body that contains it and goes out again. But because I have a sense of danger I am kept from going out too far, being lost in the paper if I'm writing.

I need to be where I am. When I'm not, when I'm lost

out there somewhere, I am alienated from my life and all my thoughts and feelings take place in dreams—whether pleasant or unpleasant dreams doesn't matter. Simply put, if my life is to have meaning, I need to be alive inside my own skin.

Craft is a way of working to be alive inside my skin. It calls me to myself through my body through a set of specialized movements for each craft. The search for forms that correspond to natural laws involves the greatest sensitivity of feeling. And thought, often quite precise mathematical thought (for example, in sewing), calls to the mental part not to be idle. All of this involves the craftsman in an exchange with the world outside himself in which he gives his attention fully to the task at hand and receives himself. In this lies the meaning of action—I have to give outside in order to receive inside. The one without the other is meaningless.

I t is clearly the craft product, although not it alone, that distinguishes craft from the multitude of other activities also requiring attentiveness—sweeping a floor, dusting, rewiring a lamp, or just walking across a room. The product tempts us. We either take it too seriously, allow it to claim us, to act as the sole focus of our efforts, or we don't take it seriously enough. Crafts are a perilous sort of bridge between action and contemplation and nowhere is this more apparent than in the confusion with which we face our results. The desire to be free from the effects of our results upon us can lead to the assertion that I *am* free. It can lead me to assert that only self-awareness matters, that the product is unimportant. And while it is in many ways a true statement, it isn't true for me. The self that I lay claim to in speaking of self-awareness is partial, restricted; it doesn't, for example, include the product and all my reactions to it. The self that I refer to is like looking through a peephole—the field of vision is very narrow. This pot, this weaving, this carving, exist not only in the mind but outside it as well. The product is our koan.

A craft appeals at one and the same time to the various parts that make up my disharmonious self, to mind as well as to body, demanding such extraordinary care in the service of craftsmanship that the customary self-involvement of the mind, for example, is shaken and begins to call into question its custodianship of the whole of me. Very soon in the study of pottery I realize that my thinking just gets in the way. The beginning potter, or weaver, or glassblower, then tries to leave thought out of it, to work mindlessly with the body alone. But it quickly becomes evident that when I try to "let go" in this way I am reaching "down" into the body—that is, into the *animal* body—not "up" toward the *intelligent* body. (Many craftsmen, not all of them young, persist in working this downward way, producing, not surprisingly, work that is determinedly ugly in the name of naturalness.) Of course, the thought has not gone away and is in some peculiar way responsible for the results of the idea that I can just shut off all discrimination and "allow" pure creation to take place. It's an atheistic thought, as a matter of fact, as if creation could exist in the absence of a Creator, or I could throw pots with my lower jaw slack and a foggy look in my eyes!

I have acknowledged that I cannot proceed without the

participation of thought, and yet I have to face that my thought is a hindrance. Am I using one word for more than one process? How can I approach the problem of thought itself? Probably everyone has noticed how some form of mind activity proceeds in us all the time. When I am lying in bed, relaxed, thought keeps moving, memories, snatches of songs, daydreams, keep moving in me even when I make no attempt to structure them. Thoughts flow like water, automatically, without any pattern. They begin at one place—for example, the dinner I had that night—and move on to a memory of a party I went to last week, the people there, one person in particular who reminds me of someone from my childhood, which reminds me of the house I used to live in, which reminds me of a trip I plan on taking this summer, etc. Thought moves by association. We can see, even in conversation, how we jump associatively from one subject to another associating out loud. I can't seriously call this thought. Nobody is thinking it—it just goes on by itself. Even when my associations are about serious subjects the thought itself is not serious—it is likely to follow a thought about Jesus Christ with a thought about getting the brakes on my car fixed. My associations have no discrimination—they run around like puppies with no purpose except activity. When I am working at throwing a pot, these same puppy thoughts suggest to me by association, through material in my memory triggered by suggestions of sensory perceptions, the shape of the pot. These thoughts may be harmless in themselves, but the power of the associative process itself is unmistakable; I can't stop it.

What about fixed thoughts? These do have force in my

life—my opinions, convictions, about politics, moral and ethical imperatives, judgments about people and about myself, ideas about religion, art, human behavior, right and wrong. Aren't these convictions also a form of association but one that has been repeated so often that every time I am faced with the same question the same answer will appear associatively in me? "Don't wear that blouse," I overheard a mother telling her daughter. "Blue clashes with green." Does it? Always? But if I have this little rule —if blue then not green with it—it will protect me from the offense of clashing colors; it will also protect me from *looking* at the colors and needing to be sensitive to them. Slogans, in whatever form, on whatever subject, insulate me and eliminate the necessity for new thought. Opinions are *all* old, are *all* a form of prejudice, are *all* indicative of the absence of thought. They make me, at the points at which they speak for me, invulnerable to that moment in my life, closed to it, protected from new experience. How vulnerable do I want to be? Certainly my previous experience and the lessons learned from it must not be altogether denied. I know that fire is hot and I would be stupid to put my hand into a flame as if I didn't know that I would be burned. But people will say—with the same conviction as "All fire is hot"—"All lawyers are thieves," a very different sort of statement. I have been burned (by a lawyer) and I'm afraid of being burned again. Lawyers are thieves, doctors are only in it for the money, salesmen are out to cheat you, Republicans serve the interests of big business, Democrats squander public funds, policemen take graft, hippies live like animals, car mechanics union bosses stewardesses Italians German shepherds—blondes have more fun—wool itches—do I want to live like this? How vulnerable do I want to be? Can I choose?

All these opinions are the most obvious forms of prejudice, universally acknowledged, recognizable as such. There are more subtle ones—onions don't agree with me, I can't sleep on planes, I'm afraid of spiders, I like tall women, a walk after dinner is good for you, soft music is restful, I don't open other people's mail, I believe in speaking my mind. I *act* on the basis of these opinions (or believe I do); they are true for me through repetition which reinforces them. But they are true through habit, without thought. The situation that calls them forth produces the association, the opinion, and so *I am these opinions* but these opinions are not Myself. I am protected from ever encountering Myself. At almost every moment in my life there is an association that spares me the trouble of inquiry. And indeed when a situation occurs for which I have not a ready-made habitual reaction, I am uncomfortable and will remain uncomfortable until I can find something familiar in it so that I can react in my customary way —without thought. What we call thought is mostly a hunt for the "right" opinion. It is so all-pervading that, having nothing better to compare it to, we take these fixed associative reactions for our intellect. They are all passive, that is— automatic. Active thought is creative; something new appears. But we have so little experience with the new (and such a fear of it) that we take as new what is often just a strange juxtaposition of old thoughts—a mule's head on a cat's body is not new, it's just silly. In art and craft it is what I call "innovation"—a pitcher with three spouts. If the first principle of craftsmanship is study how can I pos-

sibly study anything with all this insulating material cush-
ioning me from the shock of any real contact with life
through the mind?

There is no way in which I can be selective about the
insulation. There is too much of it and I am blind to it
because it is all around me. If I want to be free to let the
world in, the insulation has to go. This is why I ask—how
vulnerable do I want to be? The insulation *does* protect
me, at a price, the price of the absence of a free exchange
of substance between the world outside myself and the
worlds within myself. In theory, of course I choose life, I
choose heroically, at any cost, without a moment's hesita-
tion, surprised that anyone should think there would be a
question. But in *practice*, I have chosen security, protection
from life, and that should give me pause for a moment or
more, because there has to have been a reason.

I remember what it was like to be an adolescent, how
painful it was to be unsure of myself in the adult world, not
knowing how to act, what to say, not knowing who I was,
not knowing what I should do or what the forms were or
what I thought or felt. Gradually a veneer formed and I
was grateful for every bit of it because of the ease from
discomfort that it brought me. I made concessions, learned
to compromise, learned to lie to myself, and while I felt
regret for what I was giving up, I gave it up anyway and
finally I gave up my regret. I don't think that this is stating
the case too strongly. Now I propose to go back and merci-
lessly strip off the veneer of opinions, slogans, labels, forms
of thought, fixed associations, that have made my life

bearable even though they have numbed my sensibilities. Obviously it will hurt. Why go toward pain? I have to have a wish, a felt wish that is more than a thought, because I don't really trust my thoughts to be strong enough to maintain an act, and more than the sentimental tickle of my ordinary feelings (although perhaps I trust these more than I need to). I have to trust that I can have such a wish even when my thought denies it and even derides it and even when my feelings are absorbed elsewhere. This wish can be stated in different ways—to be free, to be normal, to be a real person, to be alive, to be Myself, or simply to Be—or need not be stated at all. The statement is often a distraction; the more complex it is, the more of a distraction.

The fixed associations are something like the money and keys, cigarettes and credit cards, I carry around with me. I am always prepared, so that nothing bad that I can foresee can happen to me. Life *is* dangerous; sickness, financial problems, accidents, separations, death, are always happening all around us and with all our endless preparations we are always unprepared for them. Our *thought* is unprepared because we are always preparing, always warding off the minor discomforts out of our great fear of the unexpected. Some months ago I happened, through some process of self-reasoning I don't remember, to lose temporarily my fear of running out of gasoline. Within a short space of time I ran out of gas three times, finding myself in "situations" I couldn't have allowed to happen before. The experience was liberating. I found the fear of running out of gas had been much worse than the actual experiences, which were merely inconvenient. Is it really so terrible to get lost in a strange town, to lock oneself out of the house, to have no money and have to ask a stranger for carfare? Isn't there then the possibility at least that in these minor emergencies I will need to call upon myself in a way that I hardly ever need to while following along my customary safe paths of conduct?

In the same way, if I begin to question my opinions, to ask myself if I really like what I automatically claim to like, or dislike what I always hear myself saying I dislike, if I begin really not to know, I will find myself in inner situations I would not have chosen for myself and I may be surprised by the person I meet there.

The danger is that when I glimpse my inner disorder I won't be able not to try to put myself in order, try to change myself. Having become aware that I am a tangle of opinions and therefore cannot come into touch with genuine thought, I may try to change by adding to what I see the new opinions I now have about how I should be. And I confuse the inevitable chaos that results with the organic state of not knowing. Except that nothing is born out of this chaos.

The principle of study, the active verb "to watch," originating as an external guide in my exploration of a craft, begins to mingle with my life. The question of craftsmanship is so wide, its implications for my personal life are so promising, that little by little there is a shift in my perception and instead of sensing myself moving toward the craft and into it I sense that the craft moves toward and into me. It isn't quite true, a craft isn't an entity, an intelligence, and I need to be careful about my anthropomorphizing tendencies, but what is true is that I begin to stop attacking the craft with my thought. I am accustomed to go at everything, even thinking, with the energy of my physical body. (When my body is tired or not feeling well, I can't think and my feelings become pessimistic and irritable.) This is why my thoughts while working at the craft have been a kind of attack. My thoughts, like everything else, go out, fueled by "muscle" power. Watching, on the other hand, requires a different sort of alertness, a tonus more relaxed than muscle tone. So it seems to me, in my more quiet appreciation of the task of craft, that I stand very still and watch for the craft to approach. I watch *myself* and I see, more and more, that the way I am prevents the craft from drawing nearer. The observation makes me more indirect and more subtle in my study.

All the while, of course, I continue working at my craft. Even when I am most discouraged, and the obstacle of myself seems endlessly insurmountable, I continue.

There is something else, something I've hesitated about mentioning until now, not because it isn't important but rather because I didn't know and still don't know exactly how to place its importance. I don't work at pottery alone but at a small studio with like-minded people. We each work almost always at individual projects and so in that sense each of us works alone. We have not chosen to work in the same place and mostly at the same time for the sake of convenience but, I would have to say, for the sake of inconvenience. I said that we are like-minded, choosing the word with special care, and yet there is probably no particular in which we would all agree. And this, not only in externals, in matters of technique and style, but also in our approach to the problems each of us encounters in his search for a better understanding of the meaning of craftsmanship. We disagree, richly and often, and do not often have many kind words to say about one another's finished pots—quite the opposite! We come from different backgrounds and we are not, in the usual sense, friends—we don't meet socially. For me personally our association, enduring some years, is of the utmost value. And I have many times asked myself why this is so. Maybe it's this: I have my points of view, acquired over a length of time, through struggle with the clay and with myself, certain understandings I've come to, and I am convinced of their validity. He, on the other hand, working near me, has come to quite other conclusions, as reflected more in the way he goes about his work than in his words—we are mostly too busy to talk much—and I respect him, the quality of his seriousness and the effort he has been making to understand. It puts my conclusions in question and points up the far greater reality and worth of the struggle, which we share, than the conclusions we don't share.

Another aspect, revealing a positive side to a rather ridiculous part of human psychology, is that I work differently with other people around me than when I am alone. There is a certain tension, not all bad, in knowing that someone else can come to an unpleasant judgment about me because of the way I work. He may think about me, "Ha, look how much she had to trim off that pot, what a sloppy worker!" Not that he *would* think it (if he did, he would have sacrificed his attention to his own work), but that *if* he did, he would be right and I would be ashamed.

Because of the possibility of other eyes upon me, I *become* an Other, looking at my work, and it helps me to remember. The actual possibility of being seen helps me to see. It helps me to lie to myself less and if, in the process, I invent a new series of lies, if, because of the tension of other human lives around me, I play to an audience in my work, I will have to see that too. There is a constant struggle for balance, for the right tension. Since in the major part of our lives we either are actively with other people or have them in our thoughts, it seems to me almost artificial to isolate myself in my work. And yet, sometimes when I have the studio to myself it seems to me that I am more able—to sit quietly in front of a pot trying to understand how the surface of it needs to be treated, to move more freely from one part of the room to another without being distracted by another's field of force—but without others, without the distractions and the fear of judgment, the human question would not have been able to enter in so lively a fashion into the arena of my study.

The human question, the question of my feelings, is in many ways the most difficult question anyone has to face. My feelings are always being called into reaction when I'm with other people. And there is no way I can be dispassionate about what, by God, I am feeling right now! I have, of course, many ideas about what I *should* feel and emotional reactions to my ideas, so that my feelings are almost always a muddle of contradictory pulls and judgments, guilts and justifications. All of this activity taking place in me just because another breathing bit of tattered humanity like myself is in the same place as I and has done such and such or not done such and such! It's a wonder. It tests my substance, the material of me, and reveals me to myself as nothing else can. With other people, trying to relate to them, my isolation from the world outside my skin is much more dramatically apparent than if I betook myself to a mountain cabin to work, there perhaps to dream of the oneness of God, nature, and man, and of my growing sensitivity through working with the simple exquisite forms of pottery. Other people really complicate life for us but it's better to have real complications than imaginary simplicities. So I continue to work with others and I continue to suspect that—in the long run—it will make me better as a potter and as a person.

It isn't really that I have to learn to put up with others but that I need to learn to put up with myself, my reactions to other people. The unconscious assumption that my own ways are the standard by which every person must needs be judged is at every turn hooted down by my peers. It brings to me a wish to see more clearly how things are, not to make things easier or better or different, but to understand.

Beginning

Between the world of God's Creation and the world of man there is an atmosphere composed of objects and implements, not quite miraculous, not quite accidental, the world of imperfect creation, the world of the man-made. This world arose quite naturally, in earliest times, as the necessary response of human intelligence to the intelligence and order of Creation. The invention of the wheel and axle was inevitable as a sympathetic vibration echoing to the great wheel of the cosmos. That the wheel was needed for transportation and as the means to an easier life is not its primary cause but only the visible part of the response man, by his created nature, had to make.

Human creating is a metaphor, an analogue, of Creation. Through his activity man opened a dialogue through which he could approach more closely to an experience of the laws of Creation. The laws, ideas, spirits, personifications of forces operable on a cosmic scale were called upon to extend their influence into the very details of daily life of ancient man.

Time passed. Man the nomad hunter became farmer.

Cities appeared. The labor of the individual man became more specialized, divided and subdivided into smaller and smaller units of the totality of knowledge possible to a man. From this ever-narrowing base of knowledge objects proliferated. The sensitive atmosphere of man-made objects which had served for an exchange of energy between Nature and Man began more and more to become thick, polluted, and less light came through it. The proliferation of objects continued, more complex, more specialized, for pleasure, for comfort, for sheer cleverness, for more efficient murder, for improving a quality of life whose only referent became man himself, alienated, that is to say, unresponsive man. The medium of common understanding between man and man had been in his individual acknowledgment of and effort to experience in his life an exchange of energy between levels, between the worlds.

As man turned introspectively toward his private psychology instead of toward the more universal psychology which is the measure of his connection with another level, he substituted the pleasure of attainment for the action of the Good in his life. As he turned toward the personal he turned away from the possibility of becoming individual, a unique and functioning independently, dependent part of a greater whole. As he lost even the distinction of the difference between personal and individual, his ability to communicate with other men diminished and is at the present time all but extinguished.

Man now lives among other men and in the world of objects as a stranger. He was born into a world of objects and educated to their use through imitation. His approach to objects is almost exclusively through informational thought, and very limited. Water appears through a faucet —how it appears, from where, through pipes of what composition, does not really interest him. He washes with soap and does not know or care to know what soap is. He dries himself with a towel, made of what, made how, made where, is of no great importance. These objects are in any case not made by people but by factories. One could know how they were made, even to chemical formulas, and still have added to one's knowledge only some interesting but essentially unevocative trivia.

The connection between material and creation has been broken. The relationship to things has been forgotten. Objects no longer relate to man as an expression of his need to be in intimate communication with the vast world of forces outside himself. Objects exist only to be used— they refer back only to the man himself and stop there. The circulation, the movement, the exchange, is gone, vanished.

In the past few decades the acceleration of this process of the dissolving of connections has become so rapid that we perceive it and have become frightened by the absence of meaningful links between ourselves and the things we live among. Some of us, mainly the young—in part because the external forms of their lives have not yet become fixed and in part because their childhood dreams of great possibilities for themselves are still alive in them—have turned toward the search for a different way to live. The most definitive characteristics of youth surely are impatience, excitement, and the unwillingness to compromise. This has led some of the best of our young people to some very exaggerated life styles. The ability to think deeply and carefully about a problem requires patience. In impatient search for a better solution to the problem of living they have settled in many cases on merely a different way to live, whether better or not. They have turned toward Eastern religions, invented religions, ecological reform, American Indians, cults, communes, and crafts—all in the same spirit of trying to find real and basic values. They expect what is real to be simple and that is, I think, at the core of their misunderstanding. In rejecting the society that shaped their discontent, they reject without knowing it the human nature that shaped society and which exists in themselves as well.

A generation of people who grew up with television and TV dinners has been educated to quick and easy gratification and that is a fact which, like it or not, has to be taken into account. The study of how we actually are needs to be undertaken simultaneously with a study of what we can become. If I think I am free from the human failing of hurt feelings I won't last long in a commune and I'll wind up blaming the others. Most communes don't last long.

The approach to crafts is much the same. It is often initiated by a dissatisfaction with the "plastic" world—that is, the world which does not touch our inner life. Young people turn to pottery, to weaving, to cabinetmaking, as if the life of the craftsman were simpler, *easier*, than the life of a businessman, and, for them, it is. And yet the realization that the objects in modern life do not touch our inner life, the wish to rediscover the connectedness between the inner and the outer through working directly on a material with the body and the best of our understanding, can lead to a shattering self-discovery. It may bring upon me the weighty knowledge that the inner life I am striving to express isn't there—that I have no access to an expressible inner life. Craftsmanship begins with disillusion.

Disillusion is an extraordinarily interesting state of being, having immediate and far-reaching effects. It is a sacred state, a state that has power. It acts at once to still the voices of mere discontent. It is an active, not a reactive state, and if the craftsman can bear to stay there, not to turn away, he begins to detect an opening in himself through which he can learn.

And of course he turns away. We turn away. We never expected to be so shaken, down to the roots. We never before understood that in a real exchange we have to give up something. We visualized the world of forces as if it were a supermarket into which we could enter and fill our shopping carts and go home again. We never thought about paying.

Disillusion, the recognition that I am not what I thought I was, that I don't know what I thought I knew, that I can't do what I wish to do, is the payment that opens us to the creative dialogue. It renders the craftsman, strains him through a very fine cloth to rid him of impurities so that he, like the material substance of his craft, can be available to be worked upon.

But, unlike the simpler materials of wood, wool, or clay, he doesn't remain available. He has feelings that react, thoughts that explain. He turns away from the experience and is attracted into his reactions and explanations. He finds himself back where he started from. Except that something remains, a trace, a sort of inner tingle, because there, in that special state called disillusion in which everything is turned inside out, I know that I'm alive.

The first prerequisite for a better life or the attitude that would make for a better life would have to be that life-giving forces are recognized and appreciated by us, that we value what makes us feel alive. Could my experience of disillusion, if more deeply met, open me to a new energy in myself?

To realize intellectually that we live in the world of illusion will not of itself liberate us from our illusions. It can do quite the opposite, forming instead an overlay, a sophisticated "knowingness" at the surface, making us tell lies in the language of truth so that yet another layer is added to the onion of illusion.

The mind isn't strong enough. It is too easily beguiled, too easily fascinated. We approach craft with enthusiasm, with the desire to learn, the wish to express something real in the concrete world of objects. There is a small, very small commitment—that is, I put my money where my mouth is—I try. The effort that is put into the craft produces material results—objects. As I continue to work at the craft I become aware of interference, something that comes between me and the object even while I'm working to form it, a static that prevents the sound from being pure. So that when I look at the object its inconsistencies echo back to me this incomprehensible blockage. At first and for a long time I take this interference as incidental to the work I'm trying to do, annoying, perhaps even disheartening, but not truly significant. It is an arbitrary something that comes between what I think of as my real understanding, the feeling in me that wishes to take form, and the object. I try to brush it away as if it were a buzzing insect but I somehow never take the "time" to look at it more closely. Until I have to. Until it begins to nibble away at the corners of my self-confidence and I begin to recognize it, not only from the last hundred times it has appeared, but more essentially, I begin to recognize it as being intimately familiar. It is me.

The object looks like me, not physically but actually. I have no need to *try* to express what I am, I *can't help* expressing it. The object is a mirror, an accurate reflection. That I took so long to recognize it is a telling commentary on the fact that I don't know myself. The way I walk, the way I play cards, my relationships with other people, the way I weave or carve or throw, express me. But only in crafts is the result of that expression frozen in time and space like a still photograph, distinct and separate from myself, small enough, calling to be seen. And in crafts only those can hear the object calling to them who have tried very hard to do the thing well, who have tried to work honestly for a higher quality of craftsmanship, and who have an emotional stake in the results produced. If I don't care that much if the object is beautiful but only that I can sell it, my reward for my work is in money. But if I care, if I can be hurt, there is no way around it—I will suffer from what I see. But I *will* see—directly—and be much less dependent upon the opinions of others. This is the real work for results—to put the best of my effort and attention into the external production of craft objects, to hold nothing back, so that the expression of the partial nature of my understanding will be as rich and unequivocal as it can be.

I suffer from what I see. It, the object, contradicts my ideas, my illusions of what I should be producing and it wounds my self-love to see it. I think it should be better

and so I suffer from it. But it is me. It *could* not be better
—I have worked as well as I could, not very well but as
well as I could, and this object is the only possible truthful
representation of that work. Faced with the truth of it, I
enter the state of disillusion. I suffer it, no longer from it, I
suffer it, which means I allow it to be, I accept the truth of
it. For an instant, and then the arguments begin—it isn't
really representative of my work—I'm tired today—I
wasn't really trying—someone distracted me. The impas-
sive eloquent object remains. The voices of argument die
down. I turn toward the object and toward myself, toward
the truth, which, although it is bitter, is also, through being
true, sweet.

The beauty of the object derives from the quality of the
work that went into it, from the attention that went into it.
Technique doesn't play as big a part as we credit it with;
many, although certainly not all, of the spontaneous art
objects of children are wonderful (the less said about the
supervised art objects they produce, the better). Quality of
work is a difficult concept for us to understand. I realized
that for the first time when I saw a broken and glued-
together Chinese bowl offered at a high price. I cared, with
my Western mentality, much more that it was broken than
that it was beautiful. I wanted the *object*—intact—the
integrity of its production was not something I was able to
relate to.

The impact of the state of disillusion shakes more than
my unthinking faith in myself. It shakes up many of my
ideas, maybe all of them. So many of us wish for a better
quality of life without any understanding that we might not
at all know what better means, that better may not at all

mean more comfortable. We wish for purpose in our lives, by which we mean we want to know what the purpose is, to comprehend it, before we take the chance of living it. But the life of meaning may not be comprehensible to the static intellect; it may require for its comprehension an intelligence that is more flexible, quicker, an intelligence that we don't even have now.

Disillusion is the first appearance in us of a different level of understanding. It is not what we would think of as an emotion. The emotion of discouragement, which may follow so closely upon the presence in us of disillusion as to be indistinguishable from it, is a reaction from my customary feelings to something so new, so much a departure from what is usual for me, that I am unable to fit it into my ordinary understanding. The attempt to fit it in and the failure of that attempt cause discouragement. Discouragement signals the *rejection* of disillusion. I am discouraged by the thwarting of my need to know, to be in control. In turning away from the liberating force of disillusion I turn, in false acceptance, to the discouragement. I accept the words and ignore the music. I analyze. I try to understand with words the "harsh reality" with which discouragement colors the experience. I come to the conclusion that I'm no good as a craftsman, never will be. I berate myself for all sorts of weaknesses, both imagined and half imagined. I take the craft object which I've barely glimpsed as a reflection of myself, and look upon it as a literal portrait. Instead of allowing new knowledge to enter me, I impose the old ways of verbal invention. I invent an understanding which satisfies my need to be in control even if it makes me miserable. I continue to react, this time against being miserable, and invent reasons to be hopeful about the future. This is all quite beside the point and quite firmly entrenched in the perpetuation of illusion. The wish to know the truth, to experience truth, resists analysis.

Analytical thought, seeing not only the forest as trees but the tree as lumber, encourages what could be called "analytical" emotions, emotions that speak from so small a part of myself that they are lies—justifications and judgments based on incomplete understanding, promises that are never kept. Analysis, a breaking-down and particularizing process, a process of dissection, is best not employed on living entities.

The experience of disillusion stops thought. And with the screen of associations quieted, only then, the mind is receptive to what lies outside its own closed circle and can experience a moment of more precise knowledge.

There is the level of "normal" life and also this new level of real knowledge represented in us as the state of disillusion. From the point of view of our normal life this other level seems merely theoretical and appears not to speak to the real problems and questions of the sincere-as-he-can-be craftsman. It seems a negative approach, unnecessarily so, when what we all long for is the joyous satisfaction of feeling ourselves in harmony both within and with the world outside ourselves. It is because of our insistence on what we mean by a positive approach that it takes us so long, as craftsmen, as people, to come to the point of recognizing that it isn't getting us anywhere—the point at which we become willing to listen to another voice in ourselves.

Craftsmanship begins with disillusion. And leads, not all

at once but after many experiences, to a valuation, a respect, for the state of disillusion. Disillusion begins to be seen as a positive state, dividing—it's true—my dreams but beyond that having the effect of bringing about in my whole organism a quiet and a seriousness that unite me as nothing else has power to, and I like it.

I begin to try to bring about quiet in myself, that quiet so subtly important for my well-being. And find that I don't know how to do it; I can't directly quiet myself. I hadn't known that. I am being led, thanks to the craft, thanks to the discoveries about myself that the craft is presenting me with, along a path of self-knowledge without, up to this point, any aspirations that I would call directly spiritual or religious.

Is there a connection between a spiritual way, a Path, and crafts? I would almost hope that there isn't, because of all the dreams and misinformation I have about religiousness, mysticism, meditation, etc.—dreams and misinformation that give evidence of their existence by the fact of my opinions, pro and con.

Now that the question has raised itself I feel compelled to face it, although with a great deal of reluctance. If I approach the question historically, trying to document the use of crafts as a method used by spiritual teachings, I very quickly run into the problem of trying to determine what teachings at what stages of their existence were (are) living teachings and whether crafts, if used, were used at a more alive or more degenerate phase of the teaching. I run into the big issue of the connection between the teaching and the historical time and place at which it appeared, which surely would affect the choice of methods. I am faced by the problem, to which I am not equal, of trying to separate the real from the spurious in spiritual paths, the necessary from the accidental. I would have to determine what the aims of a real teaching are and set up criteria that would be broad enough to allow for differences between the very different spiritual leaders, and yet not so broad that false teachings would slip in, teachings that perhaps use the same words. I would have to know not only if, but *how* crafts were used and for this I would have to rely on, in most cases, the writings of people long dead, in translation from many languages, without being able to verify the "credentials" of the writers or the translators. I would have to look at craft objects that were produced by people on a spiritual path and be able to *see* them, to recognize the knowledge contained in them, which I can't do. But even then I would not be able to know if the work on crafts had produced that knowledge or if other training had produced a knowledge that was then expressed through an object. No, the question is, thankfully, unanswerable. It seems that there *can be* a connection between crafts and a Path, although how and in what and for what purpose I don't know. But, as a living question, it makes me approach my own relationship to crafts, insofar as that relationship is genuine, with a wider inner perspective.

What I am trying to understand through the study of craft has to do with connectedness. One could ask, particularly, the question: What is the connection between me and the world?—a question that can, in some form, and with different degrees of intensity, have meaning to everyone from childhood on.

The degree of intensity and, more significantly, the

duration of the intensity of this question (since intensity alone is likely to be sporadic and "nervous") are important to the craftsman. His efforts in the medium of his craft, to bring about a right understanding in himself, a way of right action, his groping efforts toward understanding and expressing something true in the objects he produces, little by little bring about a transformation in the craftsman himself. This transformation of attitude is itself the channel of connection with the larger world.

A question, like an aim, is a direction and a kind of signpost. The question and the attitude that supports it are the thoroughfare of the goal, the way of the goal. An aim has to partake of the attitude of the goal itself. The goal determines the means. It is even more intimate than that, less differentiated. The means are the atmosphere of the goal, the very emanations of the goal. The aim and what is seen as the goal, seen with partial vision as a far-off fixed point, are essentially the same, of the same "stuff." Therefore, the transformation of the attitude of the craftsman is a transformation of the craftsman himself. It affects him even in his postures, even in the degree of his physical relaxation. It is, though he might not just then realize it, the channel that connects him. His aim, his deepest question, his most heartfelt wish, that which seems to originate most personally and directly only from himself, comes as well from another level of being, calling to the place in him that echoes it.

We don't, of course, begin a craft from any such idea. We begin because we have some spare time, because we like the way wood smells or clay feels, because someone has stored a loom in our basement, for any number of semi-accidental reasons. The question of what we're doing arises only after we've begun and after we've discovered the difficulties of the craft and felt challenged by them. A question needs to be earned. We are lured and our egotistical wish to do well is aroused. Without ego, the more or less shrill assertion of my unique existence, we'd give up at the first difficulty. But ego resists failure. The character of every material expresses itself in its resistance. In glassblowing there has to be a skin formed on the outside of the melted "gather" of glass so that the breath pushing against this resistance can form the bubble; otherwise there would be no vessel. The shell around us, the skin of ego, that gets in the way of all relationship, is the nature of our materiality, the necessary resistance. We contain the pressure of repeated failure at the craft and it stretches us. We don't give up. We continue and even increase our efforts, gathering information about the craft, learning tricks of technique, working at it. It takes a certain sincerity not to be satisfied with the improved products of this much work. But effort, even wrong efforts, even straining for success, brings a result in terms of heightened intensity of feeling. And we find ourselves not able to sell out for less than what we somehow know is really possible in the craft. It leads us to question *how* we're trying and brings us full tilt into the wall of ourselves, the real obstacle. We become disillusioned by way of a route that seems circuitous but is really, given the nature of our human material, the quickest and most direct way.

Everything is interconnected, one Whole, gorgeously complex and various—huge orchestrated molecules of protein, the circulation of water through the oceans and sky of the planet, the intricate mobile of the planets and sun. In the human body each separate system and organ is so exquisitely well crafted one could write a poem in celebration of the architecture of the foot and another in homage to the kidney. The physical organism in its unified working is—miraculous. And yet, standing under, around, and within this work of Art, this Creation, I feel left out. I understand least of all things the movement of the energy of Mind and know least of all the place of my own mind-self in the total schema.

Brought by the craft to a condition that brings me into question and shakes my self-security, I turn toward myself in a new way, not knowing what I will find or how to look for it. I turn toward myself not like someone going into his house and shutting the door but like someone in a strange and dangerous new place who does not know what to expect and who has only his awakened senses to rely upon. That is, I turn toward myself not to exclude but to investigate.

The repeated failure at a craft, the failure that comes about because of the lack of correspondence between the truth that I only vaguely feel and the falsity that I express, the failure that cannot be dismissed, cannot be answered by feeling guilty or at fault, cannot be overcome by more of the same sort of efforts I've been making, the failure that is somehow more real than the type of success I had envisioned, has an effect. It wears me down, overcomes my resistance, brings me low. But unlike any other experiences of being diminished by life circumstances that I may have had, it does me no harm. The reduction to my self-esteem is uniform—it does not divide one part from another—the part that values and the part that is valued are both equally reduced. I am, if anything, more intact than before. And I find a new strength in myself coming from an unsuspected place, a new and very different sincerity that makes it possible to go on. It feels a bit like the sensation of obedience, although I couldn't say what it is I am beginning to feel obedient to. It may be that what I perceive as obedience (how strangely that word comes to our minds—with what a strange distaste) is the first thread of real connectedness, relationship with the movement of energies both within me and in the world.

Is it only in the modern world that the craftsman has to go through such a struggle to approach his craft sincerely, or did the craftsmen of former times come toward their crafts from as far away and with as twisted a gait as we do? The inner secrets of dead craftsmen have to remain secret and we, bowing to them deeply and reverentially (our society has not taught us how to bow but we know nevertheless), must turn away from them and go about our own business. Most probably it is what they did.

Weaving, Design

Weaving is the great classic symbol of the coming together and intermeshing of separate threads to make a new integrity. The loom, fixed between heaven and earth, strung with the long vertical threads of the warp, is a harp-like instrument along which the hands of the weaver stroke horizontal chords of color. The loom is made so that alternately all the odd or all the even threads of the warp can be caused to move forward, leaving room for the shuttle to dance in the space between, right to left and then left to right. The lines of the warp (that which is given) and the horizontal lines of the woof (the weaver himself, life as lived) combine to make an integument, a new tissue, born of the partnership between the unchanging and the experiential—that which never is still. The philosophical, theological, disparity between the two finds in weaving the possibility and actuality of congruence.

Oriental rugs are knotted, not woven. There is no shuttle. Each knot is individually tied on the warp threads and clipped. The craft of weaving is unimaginable without Oriental rugs; they are so numerous that they could perhaps carpet the earth with beauty and yet they are, strictly speaking, not woven, if by weaving we mean the dance of the shuttle.

What is weaving, then? It must not be farfetched to say that weaving is the attempt to bind together Law and Life —that the craft *is* that aim, although the practitioners of the craft would of course vary considerably in how they visualize what they are doing and why.

The knotting of a rug, on the other hand, is an approach to the aim quite different from weaving a rug. The knotted rug proclaims a view of life in which each instant is a distinct and separate unit. It opens up the question of time and the eternal.

The knotted rug gives expression to a view of time beyond man's view of himself, beyond the scale of human event. Each knot is a moment and each moment has a value exactly equal to the moment before and the moment after—each knot is Now. A whole rug done in the Ghiordes, or Turkish, knot, in which each knot differs from the others only in color, in which there are perhaps 86,000 knots, as many knots as there are seconds in a day, presents a view of time shattering in its impersonal statement about what we regard so personally—lived time.

The usual human view of time orients itself toward event, toward what happens and its significance to me then and in retrospect. We live in a narrow zone in which we are blind to the instant and the eon both, in which our unit of time, the minute, the hour, or the year, is on the scale of human event. The geologist, the physicist, and the astronomer are the same as we, for although they appear to deal with either minute or incredibly vast units of time, they do so in the abstract without disturbing my life-as-event, yours, or their own.

Far more reliable as a glimpse of a new way of seeing time is the impact of one's own first sight of the Grand Canyon, when, for a moment only, my whole life, myself, is seen as an instant in the life of Nature. And I experience —what? awe, wonder, a sensation of my smallness, my insignificance, or I'm uplifted by God's grandeur—different people would express it in different words but the universal factor is that I experience the *knowledge* of *scale*. Now becomes a fact for me independent of event. In the next few moments, as I turn to "share the experience" with my husband, my friend, my children, or as I try to put it into words to tell about later, as I tuck it away into one of the compartments of memory, most of the reality of the moment is lost. And as I turn back to the Grand Canyon to see again what I have just seen, it isn't there. There is no "seeing again," there is just seeing. Expectation, memory, has made an event, slowed down the inner quickness in which the instant is eternal reality.

First the sheep is sheared and let loose to grow its fleece again. The wool is thick with oil and stinks of life. It is cleaned and carded, the long strands of it combed. Then it is spun, either with a spinning wheel or by hand using a weight. The yarn is cooked in the dye pot with flowers or berries, bark or nuts or lichen. Natural dyeing is subtle; the color depends not only on the specific bark or leaf used but on the time of year and place at which it is gathered, so that it is difficult in many cases to dye a new batch of wool the shade of the last batch. Something, usually alum, is used as a mordant, to bind the color to the yarn. (It is the nature of aluminum to bind, to pucker; alumina is the ingredient in pottery that makes the glaze adhere to the pot.) A continuous warp is put up on the loom, snugly, each vertical strand having equal tension as much as possible, each strand equidistant from the strands on either side. In a finely knotted rug the warp threads are very close together—there may be as many as 400 knots to the square inch in the finished rug. The design, carefully drawn on paper and colored as the rug will be, is put in place behind the warp threads. The knotting can begin.

Well. One doesn't have to raise sheep and shear them oneself. Wool, clean and carded, can be bought. Even yarn can be bought. Natural dyes are more beautiful but there's a great range of chemically dyed yarns in quite lovely colors and the nearby department stores are well stocked with them. (I ask the indulgence of my weaver friends at this point—their shocked protests ring loud in my imagination. I am only trying to find the bones of weaving—what is really necessary beyond any doubt.) It would even be possible to use a man-made fiber instead of wool, although the finished rug would by that be made less valuable.

What is the craft of weaving and where does it begin? If craft is a process of learning, learning from inside oneself through having been through it, nothing one can learn from books or from being told, how can I know if this or that modern technique, apparatus, or shortcut cuts me off from an essential ingredient of experience? Or, through fear of cheating myself, do I have to work at a craft exactly the way people did hundreds or thousands of years ago.

before electricity, gas stoves, and the supermarket? I don't know. I don't know what influences me or how it influences me. Usually I go toward what I like, through attraction, or I go toward what I dislike through the attraction of the thought that it will be "good for me." And sometimes, by luck, I'm attracted in the right direction for the wrong reason. But in a craft, as soon as a person begins he comes, to some degree, under the influence of the laws operating in the craft itself. He may speak of "deciding" to use natural dyes, but the sight and smell and touch of the beautiful rugs he's come in contact with and been stirred by have been instrumental in deciding him. The decision is not made in the air-conditioned wasteland of the office mind, although the office mind is likely, through habit, to take credit for the decision. The weaver, if honest, may simply say that natural dyes just seem more appropriate. Appropriate to what? Why, to the craft, of course. And what is the craft of weaving? The weaver can't say and it doesn't disturb him that he can't—weaving is weaving and that's enough for him, it gives him enough to work with. Common sense begins to awaken in him—he will use natural dyes, he finds it ridiculous to think of raising sheep but he will of course buy the best wool he can find. The problems of walking the narrow path between ancient traditions and modern convenience don't concern him—because he is walking it.

The great pure vehicle of the knotted rug requires of the craftsman a patience he, as a modern man, is unlikely to have. The rug may take years to finish, years of dedication to a single intricate design, years of sitting at the loom tying the same knot over and over again, years of giving himself to one aim, that of working at the rug. The end product, the finished rug, is in the future, too far ahead to encourage him. It requires a different patience from the patience we are accustomed to—the patience of waiting. This other patience is the patience of doing, the manifestation of patience in activity, and it presents for us a psychological contradiction difficult for us to make our emotional peace with. The knotted rug came out of and belongs to a culture that supported it. The world, East as well as West, is changing. We are influenced more than we know by fast-food chains and the philosophy of immediate gratification. The people of the East who made the great rugs of the not so long ago past came to the craft from a different philosophical, religious, moral, social base. The craft of the rugs grew out of the ideas at that time and place and in turn nourished them. We are elsewhere, and how are we to approach the manifestation of ideas that are not only no longer current in the world but alien to every aspect of daily life that we can see?

In the knotted rug each knot is an instant, each instant is a moment of knowledge, each instant is myself here, real, part of a larger reality in which the personal is subordinate to the eternal. The design of the rug is the world in all its complexity seen from one or another aspect. Our lives have prepared us for the personal and the vigorous. The woven rug, a more secular vehicle, seems more suited to the modern craftsman.

Ideally the knotted rug expresses the sacred; and ideally the woven rug sacralizes the secular. In the knotted rug the life of the weaver is left behind, put aside, and in the woven rug it is brought with him to be transformed. The one vehicle is not better than the other; both are vehicles. Weaving is more varied, more vigorous, and, in execution, presents more choices and demands more skills than knotting. It offers a range of techniques that go from medieval tapestries to Navajo rugs to the kilims of the Middle East.

In the woven rug time is sensed as a phrase and the phrases come together to form the rhythms that compose the rug. In working at the rug the craftsman is always trying to find the rhythm, to allow it to come into his body so that he doesn't constantly have to go back and count how many warp threads the design calls for him to cover. It may be as simple a rhythm as three and two or much more complex; the weaver only feels himself part of the flow of the weaving when the dance is within him. And all the time he mustn't lose himself entirely in it—he has to watch, watch with his fingers and hands that the tension of each piece of yarn pulled through the warp is right, not too loose or too tight, so that the finished rug will lie flat and not buckle. He has to guard the vertical edges of the rug as if they were the edges of the flat world and he could fall off there, to keep the edges straight and even. All of this is part of the rhythm, of the dance, and his body, too, dances, changing the shed with foot and arms to bring odd or even warp threads forward, his torso swaying right and left as the yarn is laid in. For that his posture has to be correct or his back will pain him. He is always in danger of losing the dance, of making a mistake and having to go back to correct it—giving up what has ceased to be dance, and, as evidenced by the mistake, become merely momentum.

A mistake not noticed at the time may cost a day's work, four to six inches of weaving needing to be taken out, or it may be that weeks after the rug has been started he may find a mistake made in the first days of weaving and will make the difficult decision to leave it there, to live with it, like living with an infirmity, and go on.

Design is a separate question. Unless the design is "true," the aim of weaving, the intertwining of the threads of life and the laws that direct life, isn't served. The weaver produces then a rug that has no place, no meaning. He serves only his technique and not his education. The craftsman-weaver cannot withdraw from the problem by saying that he's not an artist. To say that is to make an artificial distinction between art and craft, a distinction that has been foisted upon us by the age of analysis, of separatism, and which encourages what could be called "moral deafness." It is a common illusion and a false comfort to think of art as a matter of talent. Certainly there are people who have a great facility for drawing but what they draw may not have the capacity to touch us; it may do no more than excite our intellectual admiration. A talent for design can so easily get in the way of the search for right design. The person who finds it easy to design and the person who finds it difficult are at the same level of ignorance when confronted with the question of true design. The one imagines he is able and the other imagines he is not able; both regard the question from a grounding in false principles. Design is not invention. It is sensitivity.

The beginning weaver is enthusiastic in front of the

wonderful possibilities that the field of weaving opens to him. His designs may be quite bold and free and have the charm of naïveté. He doesn't weave very well but it hardly matters. If he tries to sell his things people will buy them, responding to the freshness and exuberance that show in his weaving. Little by little the weaver becomes less charmed by his own awkward products. He doesn't quite know what's wrong and tries to make up for what he begins to sense as a lack in himself by generating a new and forced enthusiasm. He begins to weave bits of stick and other extraneous objects into his (by now) creations. He may make huge and very ugly wall hangings which he tries to persuade himself are Art. Heaven help him if the public believes it. He is lost and may become an Important Artist but the craft can no longer teach him.

It takes time to learn from the craft. After the first rush of enthusiasm, or the second, the weaver may withdraw into himself and begin to study at the loom. His designs are simple, either bands of color or geometric figures that are vaguely American Indian in feeling. He begins to *feel* something about design and he begins to have a sensation about it as if he could, when he looks at a design, taste it in his mouth and sense it with his body. His eyes convey the design to his body and if he keeps his body still while he looks he can sense the design better.

What looks good on paper may not be right for a rug. It all depends. Always while designing he feels on the edge of a secret and the secret both eludes him and lures him.

There are forms, like the cross and variations on it, that feel right on a weaving. The triangle and the triangle within a triangle are for some reason rich with meaning, even mysterious. It depends on the size of the figure relative to the size of the weaving and it depends on whether the colors cause the figure to come forward or go back. They have meaning, like music, and the meaning doesn't translate into words.

The demands of weaving that the parts of the body each do their separate jobs and that they all work together, the requirements of speed, attentiveness, sensitivity of touch, rhythm, educate the weaver so that he is able to approach the question of design with a more active attention. In every craft except for those in which design is obviously the most important element, like painting, the study of design and the work on design come later, almost too late, only after the work at the craft has educated the craftsman to wish to be able to see. Until then it is never given enough time, never taken seriously enough.

When I sit down to explore form, to search in the unknown for a design, before I place pencil to paper, I am at the center of a circle. When just one line is on the paper it is the beginning of a radius, one of an infinite number of possible radii from the center of the circle. Each beginning defines a certain limit. Once it is begun other beginnings are no longer possible. Every creation is like that, every tree and every human life as well as every design. Each one is a direction away from the center according to law.

Designing can be a process of discovering the progression of order, lawful progression. If • then ——. (It has to be; • • or • • • is the same and doesn't advance the idea.)

Once there is —— then there can be $=$ or $+$. A choice has to be made and each choice determines the following particular unique configuration of the design. If the choice is really a true one, a lawful one, the shape has meaning, the design is itself, an entity. It stands. If the choices are inappropriate, insensitive, innovative, or arbitrary, the design is lifeless. It doesn't say anything to us; it isn't *about* us.

I sit down to study about two triangles, for a design. If that's put the other way, that I sit down to make a design using two triangles, I'm defeated before I start. The human job is to study, through an activity.

I draw a triangle, △ , and put the second triangle inside it: ◬ .

The smaller triangle seems to float. It is suspended by having the space all around it evenly distributed. I know that in two colors the smaller triangle may appear to be a hole in the larger: ▲ , ◬ .

I try moving the smaller triangle down to touch the base of the larger: ◬ .

A third shape has been produced, ⩕ , one that seems discordant.

I try having the smaller triangle share the full base of the larger: ▲ .

The third shape, ⋀ , has more to do with triangles. It's "better."

What if the base of the second triangle were to extend below the base of the first? ◬ , ◬ , ◬ . Each different form is a different statement.

Two triangles can be placed side by side: ⋀⋀ .

Or interpenetrated: ⋀⋀ , so that a third triangle appears.

Or: ◿◺ .

Their bases can almost touch: △̽▽ . ◁▷ is different.

The bases can interpenetrate: ⬗▷ , ✡ .

Or the apexes: ⋈, ⋈.

As I explore the possibilities of these two simple shapes I find myself attracted by several of them. Actually the first time there was something interesting on the paper, I wanted to choose that one, to make a design using it. But I continued, and now, with so many combinations to choose from I find myself confused, almost discouraged. What is meaning in form? Where does form come from?

One of the forms that appeared using two triangles was the Star of David. Two triangles, interpenetrated, their apexes in opposite directions, producing in addition six smaller triangles and a hexagon, a figure that for all of us in the Judeo-Christian world has associations. Taken as a design alone it is quite beautiful and, because new and corresponding shapes appear within it, exciting. It certainly has meaning as a design. We can be told that the design is a symbol, that it stands, among other things, for God reaching down to Man and Man reaching up to God. Does it really—that is, does it *in itself* stand for that or is the idea put upon, superimposed upon, the design? What is meaning? How does a symbol operate, how does it reach me?

Suggestibility may be the biggest curse of our lives. We are suggested to by everything—the weather, our physical condition, the shape of the room we're in—literally everything. We are *possessed* by the weather or the tone of someone's voice, swept away, lost to ourselves.

But mightn't it be that we are suggestible with the same

part of ourselves that can respond to symbol? Isn't it possible that suggestibility is a corrupt form of the sensitivity we all need?

Perhaps we are, as it were, coated with something like a metallic salt that makes us susceptible to all impressions, like a photographic plate. Everything reaches us in equal measure, except that, where there is a previous image, or images, the new impression is superimposed on the old, making a confused image.

The earliest impressions in life, before the dominant role of speech, were impressed on a clean photographic plate, are the strongest, and underlie all succeeding images. These came in through the body—light and dark, smell, sound, touch, shape, movement through space, color, hot and cold, taste, weight, and others, more subtle, for which we have no names. The so-called collective unconscious may derive its power from the vigor of these earliest impressions, indicating the heritage, common to all people, of the body itself. These impressions have intrinsic meaning —as sensations of the body. Perhaps the unconscious is merely a modern formulation; perhaps it is the consciousness of the body, with all that is implied by body, the inner body, the presence within the body, become inaccessible to us by direct means because of the superimposed consciousness of the formulating mind.

The great attraction of art, design, form, is the wish within us to return to direct perception. The search by the artist for forms, lines, shapes, that are true, has to do with the great pleasure in turning back toward oneself, in self-reference, in listening for what is real in myself, looking for it, and observing with great joy that inside myself there is truth and the means for approaching it.

It would be misguided and an oversimplification to say that the sense impressions of infancy hold all the keys of the language of symbol. Infants perceive directly but it is that ability of the child we need, not the condition of childhood. All our lives we have been sensing creatures, capable now, if we could learn to open to them, of impressions of great and subtle complexity.

There is no abstract art, there are no abstract forms. What we call abstract is simply nonrepresentational, reduced, pared down, less bound to the associations of thought. Every form has some meaning but what we call meaning in form is order, relationship. And the great and singularly human organ for the perception of order is the mind.

What we complain about is not the mind itself but the disorder of our minds which precludes our perception of order. As the baby grows up and becomes a child he is tempted by the facility of the mind to range beyond the space enclosing the body. The mind can stretch into tomorrow, can extend into the next town, can go to China. The body and its sensations are easily left behind and more and more forgotten. But the ordering power of the mind requires real material to work with; otherwise it will get things all mixed up and work with invented and remembered images, borrowed or stolen images, indirect perceptions, at secondhand, or fifthhand—old worn-out discards. It is bad art and bad life.

Just as in weaving itself the tension of the yarn has to be exactly right, so too in designing, another sort of tension requires care. If the mind is slack, it loses the power to select, to discriminate. Associations draw us away from the problem at hand. If the mind is tense, fixed on the problem, it becomes stuck and closes off the problem so that nothing new can enter. An alert relaxed mind cannot be imposed on the mind by the mind. The mind *is* not words but it uses words—"alert," "relaxed," are words to the mind—mind alone doesn't know what they are. The body knows what relaxation is, but only when it is relaxed; it knows what tension is only when it is tense. The faculty of comparison, of degree, is in the mind.

We respond to a shape (color, size, direction of movement) with the body. It resonates in the body directly although the appreciation of the perception may be blocked by thought. When we see a design we are able sometimes to "recognize" it, although usually the mind comes in so quickly to "name" it that the perception itself is cut off at the root. But it is possible, to a limited extent, to perceive the designs of nature or of man, to be an audience.

The question we are trying to deal with here has to do with the more difficult role of creation, of originating a design that is capable of resonating in someone else as well as in myself.

Two movements are necessary. The movement inward, to universal images; the movement outward, the ordering, connecting, expressing of these images through the discriminating faculty of the mind. These two movements are akin to the two movements in weaving-as-symbol, the meshing of the vertical threads of Law with the horizontal threads of Life.

In the movement inward toward the universal we are all connected, sourced at the center of a circle of infinite radii, infinite possible creations, the brotherhood of man. In the movement outward we are all separate, having grown, through our vastly differing experiences, more and more disparate, having different thoughts, different opinions. A point on the outside of the circle may be very far away from another point on the circumference. Communication between quite different people, of different types, heredity, and backgrounds, is impossible if the communication must take place along the circumference of the circle. But a creation, a design or a person, can have integrity, can bear witness to a lawful process. A design can be truly original. A person can be truly an individual. It depends on the connection with the motive force at the center not having been severed at some point in the process of development. If when I am designing I lose touch with the vision or the force that I began with, the contact with something real, the design then grows by itself, becomes a runaway, and while the result may appeal to some people the appeal is to excitement, to anarchy, to that part in us that resists intelligence.

There are two movements. The simultaneity of the two movements in opposite "directions" is a third element, comprehensible as words but almost impossible to experience.

The image of the circle—radii, circumference—is a representation of something real, a picturing of this something. The *movement toward* what we have called the center, or the source, *is* the center. The movement "away," "outward" or "downward," in subjective space (the words "out" and "down" having meaning in sensory terms) *is* the radius. This is important because it changes the emphasis from the starting point or end point in the process to the process itself. It is a higher dimension, from point to line. In human terms it means that a movement toward the center is more true to the idea of center than any "place" could be. It means that a question (of course of the right sort) has more vitality than an answer.

If we add to this the next dimension, the simultaneous movement in two directions, it would become necessary to say both that there is no movement and that everything is movement. But it isn't sensible to dwell on what the mind can only perceive as paradox. Our minds are only too happy to play with paradoxical ideas like No-Mind. It takes us too far from the actual problem—the conflict between my scattered self and my wish to discover universal forms that can connect me both within myself and to people and processes outside myself.

"Inspiration" has fallen out of fashion. "Vision" has been left to the visionaries, people with a mystical frame of mind who produce design through some sort of mumbo jumbo, inducing a trancelike state that takes them away from the world the rest of us inhabit. But a "vision" may be exactly the correct term, the scientifically right term, to refer to a possible result of a moment in which the movement toward the universal and the movement toward the particular are experienced simultaneously.

In dreams at night we see images, the result of the discharge of emotional energies sidetracked during the day, an attempt to release the tensions stored up (to be blunt) by a day of lying to ourselves. Dream images are fairly primitive and, generally speaking, of a negative cast, the attempt to heal a breach in myself. These images exist during the day below the strata of my awareness, influencing me and suggesting to me, but unable to break through in most mentally stable people while the mind is busy.

An image thrown upon the screen of ordinary visibility from the consciousness generally hidden from us is not a simple transposition. The language of the mind is logical, linear, has to do with spatial and temporal limits, the separations between distinct entities. The other "mind," or "ground," what I am resisting calling the subconscious, has to do with forces, connections, relativity, meanings, the passages between. It does not recognize "things." An image from that "mind" is the expression of—a relationship perhaps, a kind of force. The formulating mind takes the image and makes it into a thought about some "thing," as if one object, the object envisioned, could "stand for" something else. The two languages, the two minds, are incommensurable.

For example: Those concerned about the extinction of certain species of animals and plants from the earth directly regret the loss of the animals and plants, and object on moral grounds to mankind's use of the planet solely to serve its own selfish ends. I think this is a fair statement. It is possible to look upon the extinction of species from a different point of view. Let us accept for a moment the idea that everything is a symbol and that animals in themselves are nothing but the expressions in flesh of principles or forces made visible, each necessary as the expression of that force, placed on earth by Intelligence. If lions, to be exaggeratedly simplistic about forces, personify an aspect of the principle of courage, then if lions no longer exist this aspect of courage and its expression upon the earth vanish, no longer exist. It may be that each species of animal or plant, each mineral formation, is such an expression, placed here for Man. And that Man himself has a purpose, not the least part of which is to be available to the emanations generated by the animals, plants, minerals, on the earth, that this is part of his "food." It may be, moreover, more truthful to say that the extinction of a species is not the cause of the disappearance of certain forces but the inevitable result of these forces already having been lost.

Another example: The mythic mind has given rise to gods and goddesses in most of the world's religions. These clearly were personifications of forces at large in the world, forces the comprehension of which was inaccessible to thought, but which could be made available, and therefore helpful, through personification. Apollo, god of music and medicine, drove the chariot of the Sun across the sky. We can well imagine that this good means sometimes failed in its purpose when people took only literally what had been intended mythically. And that for this reason, in Judaism and in Islam, the making of a graven image was strictly forbidden.

Christianity has permitted the image but limited its scope to the human figure, using, in the case in which the implication of a personified force is intended, the halo to indicate that the figure is more than simply a human being. The image was meant to fall simultaneously on both minds, the logical and the "other." It was originally calculated to fall equally on both, not in order to unite them, but to bring about a "flash," a kind of lightning between them, a moment of vision.

Tibetan reincarnation is the incarnation, the embodying, of an aspect, a force, of divinity. Upon the deaths of certain men the forces they had come to embody incarnated in more than one other person. A holy man may reincarnate in several other bodies those several principles that had lived through him during his life.

Artistic vision has to be "about" forces. "Artistic vision" is a fine-sounding expression but if we examine it more closely we come up against the contradiction, or seeming contradiction, that makes real artistic vision so rare a phenomenon. Art is intentional. It is the root of such words as "artifice," "artificial," "artisan." And how shall we, how shall I whose will is too weak to carry forward a course of action on the surface of my life, how shall I who find it a monumental effort not to eat a *second* piece of chocolate cake, how shall I find the will and the unity in myself to participate in a large idea for more than a moment and to intend its expression with consistency. Communication between a common "ground" and the mind is what we have been speaking of as vision. But the mind as we know it, as we live in it, is too shifty and full of static to retain a message from the stars even if through some miracle of astronomical quiet a message does get through.

Or is it a message from the stars that I want? I keep forgetting. I keep wanting to go beyond myself. I imagine "forces" as something "out there" and forget that forces are here, are operative in the smallest details of life as well as the greatest—except that I fasten my attention on the details at the expense of responding to the forces. We need to see the universal in the particular. If we long only for the universal, it is imagination, not vision, and if we lose ourselves in the particular, it is a waste.

There needs to be a proper balance or blend of the universal and the particular. A picture of a tree that reduces the tree to its simplest forms is good only as a sign, a cartoon, a logo—without intention it is as flat as the word "tree." Its meaning is too small. An image of a tree if it is too much "this tree" may delight me with the technical virtuosity of the artist but will not make me shiver with recognition. A child's drawing, on the other hand, has sometimes a very good blend. But of course the scale is small. One feels the sincerity, the simplicity of the child-artist, but one does not feel the added power of the mind as in the great adult artists.

It is possible, although not entirely exact, to equate the universal with the body and the particular, also not exactly true, with the mind. The third thing, the vision that appears through the communication between the two, could be called real feeling. Again it is not entirely true to say this, first of all because obviously the purpose of feeling is not art or design (except perhaps in some higher sense) and secondly because we have so little experience of feeling, what could be called direct feeling, and so many "feelings," that the word "feeling" used in any context at all is bound to be misinterpreted. Yet, taken with all reservations, this formula of human mathematics—body plus mind equals feeling—is not entirely false either.

This puts us in an uneasy, what could be called an un-

safe, position. Because if it is to the slightest extent true
that the artist is a balanced man, what are we?

In Iran, the country that is still in places Persia, women
and children make most of the rugs. Often several women
work together, chattering or chanting, nursing babies,
hunched over floor looms in postures my back would find
it impossible to maintain, their fingers moving incredibly
quickly as they tie and clip, tie and clip. It is a way of life
they inherited rather than chose and they move with the
natural grace of people at home. (The rug "factories" are
different, but even in modern Iran not all rugs are made in
"factories.") The rugs are made according to the old designs and these housewife-women live their daily ordinary
lives in a milieu of extraordinary beauty and complex and
subtle order. The men go about their business, the children
play nearby, and the life of the family and of the village
includes these industrious women.

A friend of mine is a weaver. She works at home at a
loom her husband built for her. She came to weaving in
her twenties, never before having seen a loom or known
another weaver. She took a course in weaving at the local
art school and has, over the years, become more and more
deeply involved in the craft. Her house is full of books on
all aspects of weaving and she is now quite knowledgeable
about Oriental rugs, tapestries, Navajo techniques, and
natural dyeing. It had been a struggle for her to arrange
the time to work at her craft but by now she has exhibited
in several galleries and had a "one man" show—she has a
certain acclaim, her family is proud of her, and it is easier

for her to find the time to work every day. The designs she uses are her own, influenced of course by all she has seen and read, but still her own.

How shall we compare two women, both weavers, from two such separate cultures? My friend is intelligent and it is a pleasure to hear her speak about the craft that has become so important a part of her life. She has investigated Sufism through books and has visited Indian reservations to study what remains there of the craft of weaving. Her work itself is very much a part of her modern life and there is no sense in which one would say that she is living a monument to the past. Weaving has become, thanks to her persistence in working at it, a genuine part of her life, and she is, in her articulate, Western way, almost as unselfconscious about it as the Iranian women are. But she is, of course, not living a tribal life. Her work is personal, self-motivated. Her life, in this culture, is the life of an artist, acceptable to this culture as such.

A woman in Iran weaves because her mother did, because it is expected of her. One cannot isolate her from her life-as-weaver. The knotting began when she was very young and is part of the formation of the way she moves and probably of the way she thinks and feels. The craft gave her much of the life she gives to it. Composed though it is of the discrete pulsebeats of the separate knots, the time span in which we must think of her as weaver is very long and goes well beyond an individual life.

The life in craft within a tribal setting is the life of the tribe. The individual life, speaking generally, grows out of it as a branch from a central tree trunk. The health of the tree comes from its roots in the traditional forms and the nutrients each leaf garners for the good of the organic whole. The tree grows as a whole and the good that comes to each of its members comes as part of the common good.

We are individualists. Therefore, for us, craft is a way of finding one's individuality. Through discovery of the inadequacy of what we think of as our individuality, how partial, how constricted, how lacking in force, how disconnected and discontinuous it is, through a process of disillusion with ourselves, we set out to find a different kind of selfhood. Our egos have implanted in us, for good or ill, the need for a self, planted it in the illusion that we have one and that it is precious. My friend's search is not less valid for being energetic and personal.

The Iranian woman is engaged in what must be called Practice. The methods she uses *and* the designs are all given. She practices them, repeats them, like reciting a catechism, more mechanically than not, not knowing why or feeling the need to know. Over the course of years, or of centuries, she becomes them. It is a way toward balance that bypasses the Western concept of the mind, and our emphasis on the mind.

What I am calling Western is not exclusively a geographical location but a psychological orientation. It exists as well in the East, in Japan particularly. One could even say that there is a westerly movement in Asia, and an easterly movement in the United States (although it is somewhat clumsily attempted in both places).

It is best to keep the orientation formed in childhood, since all the force of the person is concentrated there, best not to try to dispose of one's inheritance.

The crafts we work at here in America are not really

traditional crafts since it is not traditional that we work at them. They are repositories of traditional knowledge but for us they are new. We need to discover not the ancient "texts" themselves but the "language," the understanding, that made them possible.

Our lack is not the mythic mind—universal mind is universal—but lack of receptivity to it. Our error is not the outer-directed, confrontative mind itself, but overemphasis on it. We envy the Iranian woman her closeness to traditional life but perhaps in her the passive-receptive mind is overemphasized. For vision to occur, and clearly that is what we all want and need, *both* movements are necessary.

Woodcarving

The most interesting thing about wood for me is that it has a grain, as people do. That is, each piece of wood has a personality and, as we know from our relationships with people—trying to work with them, live with them—personality could almost be defined by the way resistance (to what I want) is expressed in it. In wood the recalcitrance of the grain, little whorls and eddies like cowlicks that won't be combed down, the fixed expressions of its accustomed shape, give each piece of wood its own face. Resistance is only resistance, however, in reaction to a force brought to bear on it—there would be no resistance if I weren't there chopping away with chisel and mallet. Everyone is easy to get along with if you let him have his own way, but there is no relationship without difficulties. In like manner the wood resists *me*, it resists my plans for it, and it does so in a way that is particular to it, so that the relationship is always personal.

The similarities between wood and people do exist but the scale is quite different. My reactions, my ways of dealing with the problems that arise, take place in miniature, so that although I can even get angry with a board on which I'm trying to chip out a design, I can't get as angry as I can at another human being, and I will inevitably feel foolish about it. The wood resists me but it cannot initiate difficulties that engage my own resistance and that in a way is its limitation as a useful psychological means. On the other hand, the miniaturization of my reactions gives me a greater scope for studying them than I have in the rough and tumble of human interaction when all of myself becomes absorbed into a reaction.

Wood is a fixed complexity. In psychological terms it presents to the carver a kind of stubbornness. We are complex and not static. In the relationship with wood we generate enough difficulties on our own to compensate for the stubborn passivity of wood. In saying this I am reassuring myself as a potter, accustomed to a plastic material that varies in its plasticity with the amount of water it contains. Wood is a new and different material for me, almost shockingly inert. How strange it is that wood comes from the living matter of a living being. What is the connection between man and tree? I have worked with wood too little to do more than acknowledge the mystery of this connection, scarcely enough to begin to sense, to feel, really, the depth of the connection. It needs to be said, whether we speak of it directly or not, that there is a deeper and more intense level of work with wood, one that can touch closer to an understanding of life in its unitive diversity, a kind of cosmology of life. But for that a lifetime of dedication to the craft of wood-working is necessary, as it is necessary in any craft to stay with the one craft, extending oneself more and more into the universal mystery it contains and can reveal in the order particular to the craft.

Wherever on the planet there are trees, people have used wood to build their homes and furniture, fashion tools, make ships, and always there are small pieces left over, to play with, to explore new possibilities with. The charm of wood as a material lies partly in its availability. But its great attraction may be more in the fact that wood is a substance which contains a certain heat, the warmth of a living being. Putting aside for the moment the scientific explanation of fire as rapid oxidation, we might allow ourselves to believe that when we burn wood we do no more than release its inner heat. When we carve wood it is somehow the same; releasing to sight a life energy contained in the wood itself. We have all through our history been attracted, sometimes fatally, to the mystery of the life force. It could even be said that all of science is a response to this force in us seeking for reflection and amplification in the world.

Wood is not only available, it is also approachable—it doesn't require any knowledge or training to begin to work with it, or anything much in the way of tools. A child with a penknife can pick up a stick from the ground and begin. Carving a board is only slightly more complex than whittling. The board selected is held to a corner of a heavy table with simple clamps. The tools are knives, in different shapes, to be sure, carefully crafted and balanced, the handles formed to fit and feel best in our hands, the steel of high quality and very sharp—but recognizably knives. A mallet, made of wood, may be used to strike the end of the handle of the chisel, to chip away flakes of wood from the design. The advantage of carving over whittling is that the latter can employ only soft woods while the former has a wider entry into the great variety of types of wood.

Each type of wood has its own style. It is hard and close-grained, or tends to split easily; I choose the difficulties I can live with, insist on the qualities I find most necessary, very like the way I choose my friends. The difference is that in the case of wood I am aware of choosing, although not really aware of the qualities in myself that cause the choice.

Each type of wood, basswood, cherry, ash, the different sorts of mahogany, has, within what might be called its hereditary nature, another nature, the environmental nature determined by the conditions in which the tree grew and the place of this particular piece of wood in the body of the living tree. The tension of supporting a massive limb will compress the wood cells at the base of the joint and make wood taken from that part dense and heavy. The craftsman cannot ignore the fact that the wood he uses comes from a tree; the wood itself will not let him forget for long.

The board, clamped to the table, awaited me. I had come to learn about carving and accepted the board given to me—it was Philippine mahogany, a material of a rather coarse, ungenerous nature, splintery and difficult to carve, but I didn't know that yet. I accepted also the design that was given me to carve, a bunch of grapes and a grape leaf. The wood is flat, the grain running flat along a horizontal plane, the design all curves and roundness, and I was there to learn to reconcile them. I used carbon paper to trace the design on the board, then drew a pencil line around the design, a quarter inch away. A straight chisel deepened the drawn line, the first time steel touched the wood. A gouge, with a shallow curve in it, was used to chip wood away, working toward the design. The line around the design prevented the gouge from cutting too close. The tool is held in the left hand, the mallet in the right, and the positions of the hands keep changing as, standing (or sitting) in one place, one cuts to the left, toward oneself, to the right, and away from oneself, working one's way around the design. At every cut I found little differences in the response of the wood. In some places the cut, aligned with the grain, was easy, the wood chipping away smoothly, in others the wood threatened to splinter and the cut was rough and looked furry. I had to coax it there, taking more and shallower cuts, varying the angle of the cut, being sensitive to the requirements of the grain, like a sailboat tacking into the wind. It can't all be done at once and I needed to go around the design a few times, deepening the trough around the design each time, sometimes taking the time to deepen the vertical cut that acted as a stop for the gouge.

The force with which the mallet is applied to the tool varies. Sometimes the area being worked on is not a sensitive one and it would be a waste of time to be tentative; one can whack away quite freely and let the chips fly. But as one gets deeper into the wood, or closer to the fine detail of the design, the use of the mallet is gentler; the board could easily become no longer able to tolerate the strain and split, spoiling the design. It requires patience and care.

Every material—clay, yarn, metal, glass, and wood too —has a tolerance, is workable only up to a certain point and beyond that point will break down essentially. The craftsman's job is to investigate that tolerance, to stretch the limits of the material, come as close as he can to the edge of ruin and stop there. Then the finished piece will "sing" like a taut wire. This is true only if the design is authentic; otherwise it is half-craftsmanship, only a tour de force, a product without heart, more preening than craftsmanship. It is as if the honorable craftsman in his journey of exploration of the material asks, "What can this wood, this clay, this glass, do?" instead of "What can I do with it?" For that he has to listen to the material, entreat it, support it where it needs support, and be tough and demanding with himself, even more demanding than he is with the material. This listening requires his most exacting attention. If his mind wanders, his hands holding the tool will stray. He will hit the wood too hard, or gouge too deeply or at the wrong angle. The wood, abandoned, without the support of human mind, will become "discouraged" and the product will fail. Most carvers do make use of a glue pot, to glue back parts cut off by mistake, but attention is a stronger glue.

I was shown the right tool to use and began to outline the grapes. The design began to emerge. Something started to disturb me then, a peculiar little tugging at my mental sleeve. Aside from a certain rather narcissistic pleasure in working with my hands, the job didn't satisfy me. I was, if I could admit it to myself, somewhat bored. I have a good deal invested in a self-image that proclaims that I love crafts; perhaps it is even relatively true. But to fall back in complacency on this affinity of mine, to predetermine, on the basis of an old observation, that since I am working at a craft I must be savoring it, is to build falsity on the foundation of truth. In fact I was not very interested in what I was doing. Why not? And why did I imagine that I should be? Had I invented a religion for myself, made something moral and praiseworthy of the struggle for self-knowledge through working with materials? Because if I had, the need for self-knowledge had been abandoned, unnoticed, along the way. It is like the housewife who begins, out of love for her family, to keep the house clean for them and proceeds by unnoticed stages to clean the house as if it were an end in itself and to subordinate her family's comfort to the imperative of a clean house—or the doe rabbit who obeys her instinct to keep the nest clean by eating her newborn brood. If the virtue of crafts is that it shows us ourselves in the moment, as we are, and we make out of them a Virtue behind which to conceal ourselves—well then, we have less than we began with. So, I was mildly bored. Why not? A good part of work at any craft is routine. Is craft so holy in my imagination, have I fallen so far in the modern sentimentalizing of crafts that I cannot admit to a little boredom?

Now, let's look a little closer. Having reasoned with myself so that I was able to allow myself to recognize a degree of disinterest in what I was doing, the outlining of the grapes on the board with a tool, I was quite ready to reassure myself that boredom is only to be expected and completely all right. In other words, to become complacent and almost self-congratulatory about "having the freedom" to permit myself boredom. Not so fast. There remains a little question—why am I bored? True, the work is not especially demanding; true, there is much in crafts that is routine, but does it necessarily follow that boredom is an authentic reaction to routine? I don't think so. I'm rather sure that it is *never* an authentic reaction. But in this particular instance I had been working at something I had never done before, not routine for me—there was something suspicious about my disinterest, which had, in any case, more of the flavor of dissatisfaction than it did of ennui.

Of course, the grapes were not my own design. And that was the answer. The ego, the ever-present, all-pervading devil of an ego. It wasn't my design. I hadn't drawn it or even selected it from a book, so I didn't really care about it. I started to imagine a design I might like to carve —a jungle cat, both head and tail extended flat along the line of the backbone, hip bones and shoulder joints echoing each other, a sense of ingathering power increased by the stylized pose. I felt how I was called by the desire to carve it, how I would take pleasure in carving it, how I would tilt my head to look at the carving as the figure started to appear out of the wood. And I had to laugh a little, inwardly, as I returned to the modest grapes. Dear ego, thou art so predictable.

Well, the ego has to be taken into account. If we ignore it or pretend it shouldn't be there, it will be there all the same, perhaps in disguise, surreptitiously pulling the strings. If we go so far as to welcome it in the name of honesty, it will come roaring into the studio like a wind and even make a moral imperative of its presence. How to allow the ego, give the devil his due, without being naïve in one way or another. Everyone's problem, something to live with; the struggle for balance.

People work well only when their interest is drawn, in one way or another, to the job at hand. My interest, I find, is attracted by the sensory pleasure of handling a tactilely satisfying material, or the intricacies of a problem that engages my mind, sometimes by looking forward to the finished product, sometimes by a kind of soothing repetitious movement, in all cases involving a personal pleasure now or in anticipation. And, let's face it, all of that is ego-based. The ego has fallen into bad odor in our time. We keep trying to get away from it and even look upon crafts as a means for learning to work selflessly. I think we have in the back of our minds the image of the monk-craftsman spending years on icons or illuminated manuscripts, all for the glory of God. And it may be true that, in some cases, the ego of the monk was not as actively engaged as our own in the work that his hands were occupied with. It is probably safe to assume that, again, in most cases, if his ego was not so involved in his physical work it was because it was occupied elsewhere, possibly in his devotions, that it had not simply disappeared. The austerities of the monk, physical austerities of deprivation of food and sleep and long hours of prayer, the emotional austerity of obedience, all were for the purpose of taming the ego, of bringing about in him a "something else" which could integrate the ego so that it might become subordinate to a more intelligent force. That intelligent force is also called "ego," but in Latin, and means "I." It is interesting that Sublime Intelligence and its most contradictory-seeming analogue are called by the same name; the Self that emanates from God and the self that is me at my stupidest are distinguished from one another by a mere capitalization. It makes one wonder if a mistake has been made. Because if the intent of the similarity is correct, it means there is a connection between "I am" (if I could become my authentic self) and what is called in religious terms "the will of God."

I bring all of this in now because I think that when we

imagine that our petty egos can be contained by the simple pleasurable work at crafts we make a gross error in the size of the problem. We can learn, through work at crafts, how the ego enters into all our activities and perhaps learn to take it into account, something like keeping a wolf as a pet, keeping it well fed so that it doesn't turn upon us.

People who have approached crafts as a way of coming to more direct values, a better way of life, see crafts, and I do too, as a positive value in their lives. But we need to take careful note of the fact that most of us enjoy crafts in part because in the relationship with wood or other material we approach this relationship alone, as our own boss, following through on our own exploration, following our own ideas. And I have learned that whenever I'm my own boss the ego is the main stockholder, the silent partner.

Egoistic manifestations are attracted by the work at crafts; most artists, craftsmen, are engaged either in the more obvious forms of self-display or in the more subtle displaying of the seriousness of their study, their dedication, etc. But crafts *are* a good way of coming across the ego, good because crafts can be, although not automatically, a genuine path, a way of getting somewhere in our understanding.

So, what is ego and what isn't? I insist on doing things my own way, in my own style, for my own satisfaction, and this, I begin to realize, impedes the growth of understanding. It isn't my style that gets in the way, it is the insistence. What is my own style, my own way of expressing what I know and learning more? Ego keeps me from finding it, keeps me from seeing through to what is real in myself, unique, even original, and offers instead the acquired means I use to insure my local and limited security.

What is real in me connects me, relates me to a larger reality; what is egoistic isolates me. So the ego is "bad" only because it's too small, too partial, too narrow, leaves too much out, is too restrictive. It isn't false in speaking —its falseness consists in speaking for the whole of myself. The world is a bigger place than ego ever lets me know. It is like a protective mother, keeping us safe, warm and dry, defending us from possible harm, indulging our weaknesses, catering to our whims, preventing us from growing up. "Mother" is the symbol of the principle of denial, "Father" the symbol of the principle of affirmation. I think it was put this way, symbolized in such strong emotional terms, so that we would not be tempted to cast out of ourselves either the one or the other aspect of our nature. "Mother" is given, in principle, but "Father" needs to be sought—as in so many myths from so many cultures.

The first step in getting what one wants is knowing what one wants. In short, an aim. Usually there is a grand conception, very far ahead, only dimly understood, and a smaller goal much closer at hand. The larger aim is not an end point, a destination, although it is often mistakenly thought to be. It is an orientation. Only if it is understood in this way can the larger aim become operative in our small aims. My small goal was to understand as much as I could learn about working with wood in a short space of time through the actual practice of the craft of woodcarving. An aim of this sort, even put into simple words, is a kind of strengthening factor that keeps one safe (more or less) from the inevitable inroads of distraction. The first distraction was, as I've said, an ego-inspired dissatisfaction with the fairly simple job of outlining the grapes. I managed to bring myself back, to keep at it. The next job, difficult for the novice, was rounding the grapes. It presents difficulties because the tool, instead of being held for a simple cut, is gradually lifted at the handle so that the metal will bite deeper at the end of the cut than it does at the beginning. This requires some coordination of the two hands, the one holding the tool and the other striking the base of the handle with a mallet. The point of the difficulty is not in the physical movement, which through repetition becomes possible and rather pleasurable, but in changing the habit that the mind has gotten into. The mind, my mind at least, is a great generalizer. If I do something one way a few times, my mind comes to the conclusion that this way, and only this way, is the right way. Even in so small an adjustment as this I could sense the mind "sticking" for a few moments before it was able to relinquish its recently acquired "knowledge."

The grapes became rounder and were undercut so that they would seem to stand out from the board. In one place I cut too much away between grapes and invented a grape stem to fill the gap. What a little focus of interest that became! On the one hand—failure, a mistake. On the other hand—the clever solution. I liked it, admired the grape stem; it was mine, my own little touch. When I put the carving away at the end of the lesson I was pleased and when I came back the next time I was pleased all over again. It had finally become possible for me to distinguish my carving from all the others without having to check for my name on the back of the board to be sure. The ego is so silly but burns with so bright a flame one has to try to look at it from a different point of view, as a source of really impressive energy. But energy for what? In any case, I knew I would return for the next lesson.

The instructor urged me to leave the grapes and begin on the leaf at the top of the design. I agreed but made a private resolve to come back to them later. I wanted "my" grapes to be very finished, very round and smooth, and the pretty little grape stem to be more carefully articulated. I laugh at myself but there is in the laughter as much embarrassment as there is humor. One sets out on a journey, stops off for a day or so in a small town, and catches oneself rooting for the "home" team.

The leaf is more intricate than the grapes, the curves more varied, and it required a greater array of tools to outline them. When it came to removing the wood from a tiny deep area and I had to use a very small gouge, I put the mallet aside and worked with the blade in my right hand. I found I liked it, whittling, and, the wood being not too hard, I was able to continue with this method some of the time. There is the problem of using sufficient pressure to cut through the wood without using so much that the tool goes out of control and cuts more than is intended. I liked that too. The tool is held differently, sometimes in both hands, and the contact with the wood seemed to me more immediate. Sometimes I held the tool in my left hand and used the right as a mallet, tapping on the end of the tool. The variety of hand positions pleased me.

I took refuge in these simple pleasures, the pleasure also in the way my thought was planning—whether to cut away the top of the leaf first or undercut the sides first, deciding on the basis of which would create the least stress on the wood. This kind of absorption in what I'm doing is what in my simpler moments I think of as craftsmanship and I like it very much.

Sometimes though, fine and satisfying as that experience is, perhaps because it is, a deeper need is touched. A voice cries out in me: Is that all there is, just this? The voice comes, I think, from a hunger for a more inclusive experience and filters up (or down) to the surface through layers of impatience and fear and other such distorting lenses. What appears from the depths is almost always distorted and often so much at variance with what is visible that we are tempted to be "realistic," to dismiss it. Sitting before the carving, I suddenly found the question of transformation in the forefront of my mind. Because I know and love pottery best of all the crafts and because the physical, chemical transformation of clay in the fire is for me a symbolic reflection of another force, a kind of help from a higher source coming to join the craftsman in his work, I was struck by the absence of that dramatic transformation in woodcarving. I had never encountered directly the possibility that my idea of transformation might be idealistic, the idealism of requiring literal, visible transformation, the hope, no, expectation, that such transformation—as literal, as visible, as dramatic—might also take place in the craftsman. As for the existence of transformation in the world, one cannot deny it, it is a fact: caterpillar into butterfly, tadpole into frog, grass into milk. The whole earth is in a state of constant conjury. To set one's inner world apart from the possibility of transformation would be to fall into unnecessary cynicism, to give up before the battle is even joined.

What is transformation for the frog is not transformation for man; what is transformation for the clay is not transformation for wood. I had lost the principle in the appearances and it turned out I didn't understand. It also turned out that it mattered to me. Wood, it would seem, an organic substance, a kind of flesh, is higher than clay, just as man is a higher creature than a frog. Is it only in the lower material that transformation is given automatically, as part of the package so to speak? And how, then, does the principle of transformation act through a material when that action is not mechanical and therefore not inevitable?

Hard questions, and here in the sunshine at the carving table, I almost turned them out as so many demons tempting me away from the Eden of the moment. But there was already discord in Paradise—they wouldn't leave. God molded man out of clay and breathed life (fire) into him. Perhaps the transformation that could be given already has been and what we are trying to understand is a second and voluntary—that is, intelligent—transformation.

Everything changes and goes on changing, and sometimes changes back to what it was and sometimes the change is in a gradual line of progression that doesn't reverse. The wood is changed, permanently, by the action upon it of the carver and his tools. But change, even permanent change, is different from transformation, and while it would be difficult to define or to explain what the difference is, we recognize that it is a real one and, except in borderline cases, unmistakable.

I looked at my carving, three quarters done; I could already see how it would be when it was finished. It was obviously the work of an amateur although nicely done. I had worked on the wood, changed it; it was in a sense "better" than it had been before I started, perhaps even more "intelligent," but it seemed stuck in a kind of purgatory, neither just a hunk of wood nor a new life, Alice trapped halfway through the Looking Glass. I thought of Pinocchio, a carved puppet brought to life through love. These grapes if through some foolish miracle transformed into real grapes would ooze not grape juice but resin. They didn't look enough like grapes and certainly, on the plane of feeling (where they needn't be representational to be real), they lacked conviction. The carving looked exactly like what it was, a learner's piece, a practice piece, and it was nothing to regret.

Perhaps this attempt of mine to understand transformation as a principle and in its application, again as principle, to woodcarving, is too simplistic. The frog, the butterfly, the fired piece of pottery, are visibly transformed, but can it be that the visible transformation is only part, and not the greatest part, of the action of the principle of transformation? Is there another way to examine the question? Because if I insist on visible evidence for proof of transformation I will be able to accept as transformed only the most sublime products of the craft, and will be left, in any case, with an unresolvable question, the transformation of the craftsman, of Man.

Within Nature every animal and plant fulfills a precise function, is a "place" on a conveyor belt that circulates the energy of the planet and through which that energy is linked with the sun, through which, no doubt, there is a larger exchange with other solar systems and other galaxies. Each organism on earth is a representation in miniature of the circulation of energy and, since laws are everywhere the same, we can infer that having witnessed the operation of this law of circulation of energy both on the level of the individual creature and on the level of the planet, it must also operate on a higher level, a grander scale.

The exchange that takes place on the earth between organisms is apparent mostly as feeding. One animal eats another and is eaten by a third. Grass "eats" sunlight and is eaten by cattle. One could say that the function and therefore the purpose of grass is to eat sunlight and be eaten by cattle. A creature is defined by, is, its place in the circulation of energy. Transformation is a change of place. The frog is different from the tadpole not only in appearance, but in function; its purpose is different; it eats different food.

A piece of pottery that has gone through the fire has a different function from raw clay—it can act as a container, can hold water. But what of the pottery that has no such practical job to do, what of the statue, what of the woodcarving? They are not removed from the force of the law —nothing can be—they can "hold" ideas, and ideas, whether perceived as thought or as feeling, are food for man.

Every creature that exists has as its function the transformation of energy and material. Man, as Toolmaker, or simply Maker, has as his function to plant and harvest, build, make, create and break down. In this he is not different from the beaver, who builds dams, or the paper wasp, the bee, the wolf who culls the weaklings from the herd of elk, or any animal who nourishes the ground with his droppings. Man is the agency through which much of the world has essential change worked upon it. This is his only job, his given place. We are likely, through our self-love, to make more of this place than we need to. Yet there is in this place no automatic provision made for the transformation of man himself.

Among lower organisms one creature is much like the other, one ant almost identical to the next—insects, fish, reptiles, birds, while they have individual differences, are remarkably alike within their species. An automatic transformation, caterpillar to butterfly, for example, includes the whole species. Mammals are more highly differentiated, more "emotional" and therefore more individual, but still, with the possible exception of pet animals, where the essential psyche has been altered by thousands of years of association with people, the differences between individual mammals of a species are far less notable than the similarities. With us the picture changes; we feel, we think, we wish, we have moments of self-awareness, needs that don't seem to fit into the great digestive cycle of Nature. Whatever the race of Man may hold in common, and it is no doubt of vast and far-reaching significance, we perceive ourselves as separate. It would seem that evolution is in the direction of individuality. For better and for worse, we are, I am, an ego, through which I perceive the world dualistically, as myself and not-myself.

One might say that the "grain" of man, the actual and potential individuality that defines him, is only what is needed, by Nature, to fulfill the function of the transformation of material on earth, that man, in spite of all his activity, is passively being used by Nature for her purposes. One could almost accept that as an idea, except that there is in us so much of the sense of individuality, far more than would be needed by Nature alone, enough left over for ourselves if we knew how to work with it.

Self-love, the individuating force, is surely the source of the necessary energy for transformation, and self-love, the same thing, is the greatest obstacle.

The craftsman, particularly the craftsman in wood, tries to work with the individual nature of the material. "Wood is perhaps the material closest to man's own temperament —infinite in its variety, vital and filled with imperfections. Each species, each tree, each limb, each trunk is an individual and should be so treated. The wood worker adjusts his pace to the individual, at times asserting his strength, at times following the needs of the materials." (Christopher Williams, *Craftsmen of Necessity*, Vintage, 1974.)

Or, written in the third century, in China: "What is esteemed in human relationships is the just estimate of another's inborn nature, and helping him to realize it. When you see a straight piece of wood, you do not want to make it into a wheel, nor do you try to make a rafter of a crooked piece, and this is because you would not want to pervert its heaven-given quality, but rather see that it finds its proper place. Now all the four classes of people have each their own occupation, in which each takes pleasure in fulfilling his own ambition. It is only the man of understanding who can comprehend all of them. In this you have only to seek within yourself to know that one may not, out of one's own preference for formal clothes, force the people of Yüeh to wear figured caps, or, because one has a preference for putrid meat, try to feed a phoenix a dead rat." (Hsi K'ang in *Anthology of Chinese Literature*, Grove Press, 1965.)

Is man of all creatures the one that has in himself the possibility of self-transformation? It would seem that the ego itself must become dedicated to the work of self-transformation for it to be possible. The principle in craftsmanship that calls us to work with materials may be the same principle which in a larger sense calls us to work with ourselves. It may be that in this larger sense, the realized Craftsman is the new man.

. . . In the center of a large carved door—Psyche, leaning, candle in hand, over the suddenly awakened Cupid. Her face expresses delight in her discovery that her husband is the beautiful God of Love himself and fear of what her transgression, in daring to look upon him, would bring. In Cupid—anger and sadness—that he must leave his bride forever, the bride to whom he had given everything luxurious and mysterious, everything except the knowledge of his identity. Psyche's jealous sisters, who had tempted her to this act in violation of her husband's one command, are carved to the left of the central figures, in their faces what is most coarse and selfish in human nature. Psyche is all fallen innocence, beauty undone by the need to know, like Eve. To the right of the two main figures, frozen in the determining moment in the history of Man, is all that must take place as a result, Psyche's journey. The whole door is spiraled around with the adventure of her search and the supernatural beings who take pity upon her on the way. Psyche, the spirit in search of Love, exhausted, disillusioned, humbled, knowing only that she must find him at any cost no matter how long it takes or where her journey takes her, suffering, sustained only by her need, through persistence and supernatural help, finds him again.

What an experience it would be to carve that door! To start with a germ of understanding of the myth and to go on, through the long process of carving it, to discover how little understanding there really is. To be on the point of giving up, and to educate oneself to understanding, through the "stations" of unremitting effort.

It may be that what we understand least about self-transformation is the scale of the efforts that are required. It is easier by far to accept the need for quiet and even to appreciate the moments in which quiet occurs, to accept them passively, even gratefully, and wait for the next time as if I had no part to play. We need to think, to watch, to find what brings these moments in which, although for so short a time, I find myself transformed. Often they occur at the conclusion of a struggle, as a result of the appearance of a courage-of-sincerity in the face of defeat. It is that courage and that sincerity which miraculously rescue us and set us on the shores of a new continent. What is it, though, that becomes quiet? . . . Well, what makes the noise? This question is the point at which effort begins.

Teaching a Craft

My daughter's class in elementary school had somehow acquired a potter's wheel, and the teacher, hearing that one of her students' mothers knew pottery, called and asked me to come in to demonstrate and to work with clay with the class. I was happy to do it. The kids were about ten years old and there was something I wanted to find out, although I wasn't very sure what it was. There was a great deal of clay in lumps in plastic bags, all of it too hard to work with on the wheel. There was no wedging table of course —I improvised with the back of a piece of oilcloth laid on a table and tried to get enough water into the clay to make it usable. The water made the clay slide around on the cloth and there was no wire to cut the ball of clay with. The table was the wrong height. All those eyes watching me! The children were quiet and I talked too much.

I took the clay, poorly wedged, to the kick wheel. I had brought a needle, a small sponge, and a rib with me, and the teacher had given me a bowl of water.

The wheel was all right, a little small but nicely made. The clay was still far too hard and the room was over-heated. The wheel didn't have as much weight in the flywheel as it might have, so I had to do a lot of kicking, and my fine pose as an adult and an experienced potter was shaken by the difficulties, minor though they were, of the situation. I was nervous. Perspiration dripped down my face as I struggled to center the clay, gathered on the tip of my nose, and dropped into the clay. I had known as soon as I came in and saw how hard the clay was that I was going to have trouble but I hadn't shared my problem with the children and then, immediately after, it was too late, I was committed within myself to keeping up a front, a competence I didn't feel.

I threw a small cylinder and then shaped a pot. The children were impressed. I felt better. I did as I had planned—as I always do in demonstrations—and, taking a needle, cut the pot on two sides from top to bottom, opening it out to show the thickness of the walls. My first teacher had done this and I continue it, not so much to show the thickness of the walls as because I remember how shocked I was that she had so easily destroyed the product of her hands and that shock and the sense of values implied by it are still for me today, when I do it, a reminder. The children were shocked—some of them were really outraged. Sitting there at the wheel, still soaking wet, I now had all of my pathetic security back. My world was right side up again.

I shouldn't have cut the pot. I did it because I had

planned it that way, because I always do it, because I wanted to share a moment of fine and meaningful illogic, because I wanted to give them something. But the slightest shred of self-inquiry in that moment would have told me that I had nothing to give. I was lost in damaged pride and cutting the pot only served to salve my vanity, to elevate me at the cost of the children I imagined I was trying to teach.

I left the wheel then and, with the help of a few of the kids, divided the clay and distributed a ball of it to each child. My idea was, as I explained to them, to begin with the right hand to shape the clay over the left, and when it began to look like something, an animal of some sort, to make it look more like that animal. I said that it needn't be any animal that anyone has ever seen, that this was simply play, that it was for fun.

Most of the children were unnerved by this. I hadn't expected it. They came to me, called to me, needing approval, wanting to know if they were doing it right, if their animal looked okay, telling me that they weren't very good at art, complaining, explaining, asking. I felt enormous pity for them, and tried to be reassuring, supporting. I tried to "persuade" them to enjoy what they were doing. I tried to "convince" them that it was fun. They kept trying to find out from me what was the "right" way, and I kept insisting that there was no right or wrong.

As I had been surprised and disturbed by my own previous nervousness I was now surprised and disturbed by theirs. My pity was external and didn't include myself. It never became compassion. I wasn't able, there didn't seem to be "time"—inner space—to acknowledge their reaction to the situation I had forced on them. I never met them where they actually were, never allowed them their human weakness, never understood.

We came to the end of it. Everyone was very cheerful, seemingly. The teacher reminded them to thank me for coming in, and I went home.

There are conclusions to be drawn from this report but it is better, I think, just to let it stand.

Almost everyone who works at a craft today was taught it, had formally or informally some or a great deal of instruction. Whether or not he read about the craft, tried to teach himself from books, almost everyone has had at least one human instructor, another craftsman, because as good as many of the books are, and some of them are excellent, there is no substitute for the help that can be given by another person.

In addition, almost everyone who works at a craft today with even moderate proficiency either has taught someone else or will in time teach. Mostly he will teach informally, that is, without getting paid for it, and often without any idea beforehand that he is going to teach or any desire to do so.

In the formal field of education, the teaching of children and young adults, teaching is regarded as a difficult and exacting profession, and its pitfalls, rewards, and methods have been exhaustively written about. The teaching of crafts, except at the grade school level, has hardly been spoken of at all. This is remarkable in view of the fact that there is a huge underground of crafts teachers, unacknowledged and uncounted, numbering in all likelihood in the millions.

The assumption seems to be that there is no special talent or understanding required to teach crafts, that all that is needed is for the teacher to know the craft well and to "show" another person how to handle the material. It is a charmingly ingenuous assumption, almost the last stronghold, in a specialist-oriented society, of a rustic ethos.

The teaching of crafts, possibly because crafts are not essential to our society except where they are sentimentally regarded as the token of a natural way of life, hasn't been worried about, isn't sanitized, denatured, homogenized, and remains almost completely unspoiled.

The practice of a craft now includes the teaching of it for so many craftsmen that we need to look at this teaching more carefully, as part of our study of craft. In the field of education teaching is often regarded as a craft in itself and I wonder if perhaps thinking of teaching in this way, as a separate entity from the material it deals with, isn't either a symptom or even a cause of the poor quality of much of modern education. Because teaching, the relationship between teacher, student, and material, is so difficult to understand, there is a tendency to simplify the problem by separating education itself from the field in which the education takes place. This separation has the effect of cutting the teacher off from a natural cycle: to receive/take in, to produce/express, to give back/transmit. When we regard education as a thing apart, we lead inevitably to the partial truth that "those who can't do, teach."

The teaching of crafts, informal as so much of it is, is

still influenced by the current attitude toward what teaching is, and suffers from it. Any attitude in the world at large, the world in which we live, is breathed in by all of us as an invisible influence on what we think and do in even our most private moments. The world we live in exemplifies an attitude toward education as a preparation for doing and a thing apart from doing. We believe this only because it has never been presented to us to believe or disbelieve—we presuppose it because it is the way we have always seen it done.

The type of teaching that fits most accurately to this attitude is what I would call instruction—the conveying of information and methods in a way that leads, as quickly as the instructor can instruct and the student can learn, to a point at which instruction can end and practice begin. Instruction can be very good, terrible, or something in between. It takes talent, care, sensitivity, effort, and knowledge to be a good instructor. It would be stupidly impractical of us, in an attempt to find a wider view of what education is, to scorn instruction. All teaching, of anything, at any level, has to include in itself a certain significant degree of instruction. Otherwise the study is too rarefied and is likely to float off into spaces so subtle that they don't exist except in the imagination.

The problem of education is the problem of continuity, the perpetuation of humankind in more than body alone. The something that is given by the teacher—what is it?

Here I have a friend, a young woman who wants to learn pottery. What does the mystery of education, of transmission, have to do with us? Isn't it enough just to give her what she came for, to show her how to work with clay, to share with her and through her the joy of exploring the texture and possibilities of a new medium? It is as much as I am able to do to remember how I hold my hands for the different stages of the process of centering, opening, and pulling up the walls, to remember and to show her; why do I feel us as actors on a small stage, part of a great unending drama under the title of "Transmission"?

Whatever teaching is, it has to cut both ways, to educate both pupil and teacher, to be full of surprises and discoveries for both, to have an emotional element, or it isn't worth the time it takes. Instruction too easily interposes a safe barrier between teacher and pupil. Bluntly put, if I have the reassurance of an established pattern of instruction, I am less likely to feel afraid. It's not a bad thing to know that I'm unsure and to teach anyway. The teaching is more likely to be alive.

We do our best, and society helps us, to smooth out the rough places in human contact. At beginnings and endings there is no momentum to cushion the contact between people—entering a room, leaving it, one is ill at ease, doesn't know how to stand or what to say. For these occasions we have formulas—hello, how do you do, we shake hands, so good to have met you, goodbye, have a nice trip. These formulas protect people from bumping up against one another, protect us all from having to acknowledge that we are full to the brim with unreasonable fear of one another. What a thing to say! But isn't it true? This fear is so much a part of our lives that we take it for granted, assume that it's normal, and do our best to cushion ourselves from the impact of it.

We don't understand relationship—people are opaque

to each other because there is such a lack of clarity in each person's relation to himself—but all these dark shapes, bundles of reactions, are constantly in motion, going in different directions, running parallel, colliding. And the energy of this activity, mostly random though it may be, a psychological Brownian movement, comes into us and then can either circulate through us a life force or, more commonly, simply pass through us, leaving us barren.

The teaching situation is perhaps the best place for all the questions of human relationship to be raised. It is the basic human relationship, more basic even than mother/child and father/child. Man and woman together perpetuate the species but the concept and the actuality of family is the beginning of civilization, the transmission from one generation to the next of what it means to be human. A generation is a sum of knowledge. It is the length of time required until a seed is able to be passed on. The mother/child relationship is sacred because it is the prime expression of the law of perpetuation and exemplifies this law in physical as well as spiritual terms: the giving of life. The mother is the first teacher.

The father's link to the child is not as physical. He is the giver of the original impulse, but his extended presence in the family is less a physical necessity than a civilizing one, more directly an expression of the subtler meaning of continuity. The father, then, although he is not the first but the second teacher, symbolizes the teacher, the carrier of the seed of knowledge.

The king, the father of his people, lawgiver, is another way of stating the basic human relationship, a symbol in the flesh. But laws have lost their meaning for us and, except in science, are equated with regulations, and the word "kingship" falls strangely on modern ears. We no longer understand with our minds the commandment to honor father and mother; although in the blood, in the deepest feelings, we still do understand.

It is difficult for me, a child of this culture, to try to place in perspective the idea of superiority without dragging in with it all the negative associations that the word now carries for me, for us. I have said that the basic human relationship, the relationship from which all other relationships derive, is that of teacher and student. The relationship between the students derives from each one's relationship with the teacher. "Teacher" is an idea, a symbol, if you will, of the Fatherhood of God, the principle of knowledge, the promise of continuity, a place, not a person. "Student" is also an idea, a place, different from "teacher" but not less honorable. The idea of the Brotherhood of Man can only come about from the idea of the Fatherhood of God. The idea of equality, brotherhood, is the direct, suprarational result of the acceptance of the idea of a level of existence superior not only to me but to all of us, the level that could be called the level of law.

We don't think of brotherhood that way any more. We think of it as a shared common purpose. When blacks, or workers, call one another "brother," it is often mainly in recognition of a common enemy. When women in the women's movement refer to one another as "sisters," it is the same—a recognition of a need all have, a burden that falls equally upon them and from which all wish to be free. Equality, when it finds us, as in the examples just stated, finds us at a level below that of other people more fortunate than ourselves; it finds us in a position of subjugation from which we hunger to be freed, and for which we unite, in a revolutionary way, against a class or order or section of society and its rules which oppress us. Which means that equality, even for modern man, carries hidden within it the idea of two levels. In the modern, perverted version, where the higher level is merely human, money or power masquerading as superiority, equality is the banding together of the weak to oppose the force of the strong, to topple the falsely superior from their position of power.

The purpose of religion in secular life was to establish in the lives of men and women the idea of true superiority, the Fatherhood of God; to establish, through service to that idea, a society of equal members, all children of God, whose relationships to one another were based on their acceptance of higher truth. Societal hierarchy is rooted in the same idea. The Father, the King or Just Ruler, the Priest, the Teacher, are all representations in flesh of the principle of Divinity. But people are stupid, greedy, and forgetful; and fathers and kings, priests and teachers, are people. Many of them identified their human selves with the suprahuman positions they held and took advantage of the power it gave them. The dam between levels broke. Societies became more and more egalitarian and the true idea of equality as deriving from a spiritualizing force was forgotten. Church and State were divided, becoming two halves on the same level of life.

Here in America, a nation founded on principles of human equality, a republic only verbally "under God," the most technologically oriented society in the world, strange things have been happening in the last decade or two.

Young people have been rebelling against the way their parents and grandparents live and have been looking for an alternative life style. They have tried to put aside the whole package of modern society and have been attempting to start again from the beginning, forming themselves into farming communes, turning to basic handcrafts, carpentry, photography; and, in amazing numbers, have become disciples in a great variety of non-Western spiritual movements. They have given up as useless all expressions of formality, and although the rejection of old formulas has inevitably produced new ones, yet the impulse has clearly been to sweep away anything that might get in the way of direct interaction—with one another and with nature. They have tried to reject conventional sexual mores, have had babies in as natural and unencumbered an environment as possible. Is there in all these different directions a common thread, an expressed need that we could recognize and to which we could respond?

The most accessible of the various modes of direct experiencing is physical, to touch, to work with one's hands, to move one's body in dance and in sports. Massage, physical encounter—a need is being expressed. The longing for direct experience, discovered in the physical world, becomes passively linked and limited to the physical world—sensation passing by imperceptible degrees into sensationalism. The emotional melodic music of a less desperate time gives way to the rhythmic hard-driving rock music of today, a music that is not so much heard as it is sensed directly with the body, a music that shakes the room with its volume. Sensation, more sensation, stronger sensation, a search going further and further down to the level of animal sensation in unconscious hope that something above will stand fast and allow or even enforce relationship between people. It has been said that today's youth are more conformist and more passive than the youth of any other period of history, that they require cult figures and authority figures. The explanation given is usually based on a more or less Freudian way of thinking about human makeup and human needs, a way of thinking itself based on the cult of scientific measurement so long ascendant in our lives.

Our hope resides in our needs. Need is truth. When thoughts about what I need are false, they give rise to the dreams by which I live, the desires, the false starts and acting out, the stupidities, the fears. Principles, laws, are real—and appear within me as needs, perceived personally as *my* needs. Needs are distorted by ignorance, bad education, and become desires. Desire breeds desire—it is not real and cannot be satisfied; the need remains and fresh desires emerge. When we find, as we do today, a large and important segment of society, the young, casting about in a frenzy, searching for how to live, we have to take it and them seriously. We have to look, not at the forms they have fastened on, but at the force that is driving them, the need that is in ourselves as well.

Whoever we are, each of us, no matter how intelligent he may be, no matter how important his position in life may be, no matter how many people depend on him, no matter how ambitious he may be, no one feels happy without someone or something above him. All of us have to feel that we are answerable, if not to a person, then to a principle, to history, to a purpose higher than ourselves. If

I am the best, the highest, the most authoritative, then surely something is very wrong. An empty space above me reflects the lack within me, and many people, not trusting that they will find a "support" above them, refuse to take on as much responsibility as they have the ability to deal with. Top executives are interesting or uninteresting in terms of the ideals or principles that they have been able to discover above themselves. There are levels in the universe; it is a true idea and the force of that idea creates a need in us to experience, on a smaller scale, levels within our own lives.

My young friend has come to me to learn a thing I have no intention of teaching her. She imagines that a craft is the objects it produces and has come to me to do what she thinks of as the craft of pottery—to make pots. She has come, in her soft, friendly way—I like this woman—bearing her invisible self-will to tell me what I shall teach her. She has turned up in a serious part of my life to undermine, in all innocence, the idea of levels, an idea of which she has no understanding and of whose very existence she has no inkling. She has come to purchase—although there is no money involved in our transaction—a commodity, to hire me to work for her, to instruct her. In this she is exactly as she must be; she could not be different. And in this she has the full confidence of her ignorance, she is unified around her casual assumption that pottery is making pots. I, on the other hand, am confused and fragmented, lacking in confidence. I have some idea of what craft is about, but sometimes I remember only with my thought and often I forget entirely. I am tempted to give in, to give her the instruction she wants and let it go at that, to give up the struggle for understanding that makes me awkward and overserious, heavy-handed, an object of ridicule in my own eyes.

The dilemma of a person who takes on the task of teaching another is here: that the student comes to be taught with some sort of fixed idea of what it is he wishes to learn and what he intends, at the end of the instruction, to know and to be able to do. In the study of anything serious the student comes for the wrong reasons and isn't able, for quite a while, to understand what the right reasons are. The student's position is very secure because what he wants is external and visible. The teacher, unless he is a master, is constantly wavering between the temptations of the visible and the elusive sweetness of another reality. The teacher, for a long time, has to practice deceit, to lie to the student, to give him enough of what the student wants to keep him coming and at the same time to give him enough of what must seem to the student unimportant to awaken eventually a different sort of interest in him, to bring him to the point at which a more or less independent study is possible.

Pottery is not about making pots. The individual crafts are all different enough to appeal differently to different people and emphasize different aspects of the world and the human approach to it. But the reason of crafts is the same. Crafts are about one thing: the secret of how to work.

Looked upon this way, the question being asked today about the place of crafts in a technological world becomes quite changed. The reasons for the question retreat into unimportance once the objects of the craft no longer occupy center stage in the consideration of what the craft is. One no longer has to reject the beauty of mass-produced objects in order to justify making objects by hand—as so many craftsmen do. A craft is not its objects; a craft is how I am when I am making them (and eventually, one would dearly hope, how I am the rest of the time, as a result of what has been transformed in me through craftsmanship). The objects of the craft are by-products, very essential by-products, of the way I work.

In teaching, another element enters the scene—the student. How do I work with her, a material much finer and more complex than the clay I'm accustomed to? Again, as in the craft, the temptation is to misplace the emphasis, to worry about how she is receiving our work together, how she is coming along—in other words, the temptation is to make an object of her, to look upon her as the object of my teaching work, and to make that the focus of my interest, doing it in the name of goodness, of caring. How do I work? It is the main thing and there is no area in which it is not the main thing. It brings the necessary third level. Two levels, student and teacher, are not enough. If I am the authority, if I have not something above myself, something to which I am answerable, a person or a principle, my teaching will be clouded with too much of my own personality. I will make demands on her that come from my convictions rather than from my search; or I will not make the necessary demands, out of tenderheartedness. For something to stand firm in me it has to be anchored, as it were, above myself.

The existence of levels in human relationship is the only answer to the fear which in every other instance clouds

and distorts a free exchange between people. The impersonal opens the space in which the personal can exist.
Among all our other fears is the fear of being "cold," of
being unfeeling, and we expend a good deal of energy on
manifesting a concern for one another that we don't really
feel at that moment, smiling, inquiring about a friend's
minor ailment, playing our part in pleasant pretense that
would indeed be harmless if it did not form the core, in
most cases, of the whole relationship. The impersonal ideal
relationship between teacher and student, student and
teacher, student and student, is far from cold. It is a reflection of the passion that binds element to element to form a
new compound—an embrace not less passionate by being
sanctioned, even demanded, by scientific law.

Mother and child—nowhere is there to be found a more
feeling relationship, and of all such relationships the arche-
type, painted again and again by serious artists, is the relationship of Mary and the Christ Child. Of all these paintings, the ones that touch us most deeply are most strangely
impersonal. The Child sits on the Mother's lap or stands by
her knee; there is space between them and a startling absence of conventional emotion. It is so unfamiliar to us
that we are almost repelled; we would be repelled, find it
cold, except that for no reason that our minds can give, the
painting can sometimes bring unexplained tears to our
eyes.

I need to be toward my student as if I were the teacher I
wish to be. And I need to be toward her as if she were
really a student. The word that comes to mind for the
impersonal space that this difficult attitude engenders is:
respect. We are actors in a play of grand design, repeating

a relationship the original of which is an Idea, and examples of which exist on the level of suns and planets, and of atoms.

Respect is an almost impossible term to think about directly. It is easy to confuse with a kind of admiration, but it isn't that. To honor someone, to look up to him, yes, but what is *self*-respect then? Why should a child respect his parents, the young respect the old? An old woman may be a fool; why should we stand up when she enters a room? Older isn't better—why should we honor the aged? "Reason" would tell us to decide each case on its merits—acting alone, "reason" would dismiss the idea of respect for a category (parent, old person) as a kind of anachronism, an old-fashioned notion that no longer applies. Thought and blind confidence in my own capacity to judge worth would make of respect just another transitory emotion, just another personal reaction. And of self-respect when given over into the care of our judgmental, uneducated reason—the less said, the better. Self-respect would either be dependent on what I think about myself, my accomplishments, my manifestations, or, worse, it would simply be assumed idealistically, equated with the rookery of self-love.

Respect is so difficult to think about because it is an idea that doesn't arise from the flat, egalitarian world in which people, presumably all equal, are all equally isolated, related only through chance, desire, and fear—our world, the only world we think we can exist in. Respect is a concept from a higher world and in a way could be said to fill the space between the worlds, to relate them to each other. Respect is, in fact, the acknowledgment of and agreement to the existence of another level, the recognition of another level. Where there are levels, there must be respect. It is a problem for our time that children, not learning respect for their parents, are thereby deprived of a means of approach to the experience of levels when they become adult.

Self-respect is the same. It is the recognition of something higher in myself, another level, my presence, that is there whenever I turn sincerely toward it. It is difficult to be sincere. All the brightly colored birds of self-love, screaming their territorial squabbles, prevent it.

Self-respect is the simultaneous recognition of my presence—and not just a vague sensation in the chest, not just the warmth of it—and a recognition of my non-being, how empty and helpless I am, how true it is that I don't know who I am or what I should do. If there is self-pity, the emptiness gets filled with it and the thoughts it brings along with it and isn't empty any more. And if there is self-satisfaction in any degree, any personal congratulation for accomplishment, it too will turn the gold to lead.

How then can there be any hope to live normally, in both worlds? How can there be relationship between levels, relationship between people, self-respect and the respect and compassion for others that arise from it? What is the force that can control the importunate emotions?

I have wondered since I was a child and first heard the term what is really meant by "the fear of God." And, as a child, reading and hearing that God is Good, I couldn't understand what this fear business was about. Surely fear indicates lack of trust, or is a reaction to power, that the power will do something bad to me, something I won't like. And as I've grown older and come to see the fear that occupies our lives, the fear that makes us stupid, that makes us afraid to reach out to one another, the fear that blunts us in all things, I've come to regard, for myself, fear as the great enemy. But I wonder now, in a world of many levels in which there is such abundance and such economy, a world in which both the rivers and the blood circulate, and planets and atoms spin, a world in which the same forces act on microcosm and macrocosm alike, a world each of whose parts could, if we could allow them, teach us; I wonder what, in such a world, we could learn from fear. I am suggesting that the fear we know, the emotional useless fear we experience, might be the dark side, the obverse, of a more noble force, also called, for reasons of true economy, fear. And, from having experienced the strength of fear in my life, I speculate that nothing less than the fear of God can keep us from closing up the space that the brief awareness of two levels brings, the space I have called respect and self-respect.

The fear of God is different from the fear of Nature. Nature is outside us and within us. God is within us and outside us. When I experience the power of Nature it is as a force outside myself. What I am calling "God" is that rarely experienced Voice of Thunder within oneself, a "voice" of such power that one is dumbfounded, awestruck, and afterward, while still shaken by it, realizes that in all activities and thoughts in daily life this most real force, this incomprehensible, plays no part at all.

My daughter glanced in casual curiosity at the paragraph I've just written and said, "I thought you were writing about crafts."

We are hungry for unity, desperate for order. Our unique treasure as humans is the gift of thought, of speech, of reason. Through words we express ideas to unify the moments of our experience. It is hard to know when the expression of an idea, even a true idea, enriches life and when, on the contrary, it becomes a substitute for life. It's hard to separate ideas as daydreams from ideas as reality. It's hard not to be trapped emotionally into the notion that the truth of an idea we've come across is the truth of ourselves. Always as we use thought to connect moments of experience we need to remember to keep them separate too.

The actual working relationships in the course of teaching a craft are so different from what I would express as my intention. Nothing ever proceeds in a straight line, and it is all so slow, so blundering and so slow.

The other day a student said to me that she had finally understood that to center the clay requires "sensitivity and firmness." Exactly right. I had not been able to find the right words in showing her, but she had persisted and found first the inner condition that made it possible for her to center and then the words to express it. I had almost despaired that she would ever be able to step sufficiently out of her "style." She is a gentle person, has been brought up in and has chosen for herself an unforceful, yielding way of being toward the world. There is strength in her but it is indirect. She carries her hands always at an angle to the forearm; I have never seen her make a gesture without the wrist bent in a posture that suggests to me submissiveness. The clay needs to be contained within the two hands, controlled; there needs to be a steadiness in the whole posture of the body, a single resolve to the inner posture. I hoped she would be able to find it in herself, and I tried to show her that this other way of facing the clay and the world is not a contradiction to the way she faces her life.

While we were working together I felt how different we were and how locked each in her own attitudes, in her own space. I felt our lack of self-understanding with a certain degree of wonder. When and how did it happen that I became like this and not the way she is? Somehow she found her own quiet way of understanding what was needed and learned to center the clay, learned even to formulate the words to tell me what she found. The small pots she has made since are very light and lovely, carefully done, the shapes simple, classically fine. Perhaps, after all, there had been an unseen exchange of understanding between us, a magical osmosis through the tough membrane separating us. I know only that I am happy for her success. I don't know and I probably will not be able to know if her experience with me and with the potter's wheel will affect her life outside the studio.

Once, weeks ago, before she had learned to center, when I was watching her unsteady hands on the clay, I shouted at her, a great burst of sound without words, and in momentary shock and surprise her hands tightened on the clay and brought it under control. It was a trick, although not a planned one, and, thinking back on it, I did not know if I should be ashamed of trying that. One is always trying to cheat time of its fullness, to find a shortcut. And yet . . .

For the teacher the consequences of his acts, words and gestures, come visibly back to him through his students. Of course it is true for everyone that each act, even each thought, has an effect, a consequence, but it is often not visible to him. The teacher, however, takes a measure of responsibility for his students and has in them, if he wishes, a mirror that reflects him. Responsibility has been variously defined, but for me it seems a very simple thing although almost impossible to live. It means to me only this: to be responsible is to accept the consequences of one's acts, even when the consequences are overwhelmingly disproportionate to the seeming insignificance of the act. A moment of inattention and someone can be injured, a joke when seriousness is called for or vice versa, a wrong word, and everything can be lost for a long time, perhaps forever. No one is always alert, always aware, even at those moments at which he most wishes to be. Often one does not know what to do or say and makes a mistake. Responsibility only means that one allows the results to come home to oneself.

A child can "take it back," can be sorry and be forgiven, can "do it over." A child is not responsible. A grown-up is responsible for himself—for *all* his consequences, whether visible to him or not—and if he imagines he is not, then he is not grown-up, whatever his age may be.

Consequences can be good as well as bad. Sometimes one is at the right place at the right time, by accident, and it changes one's life for the better. Sometimes one cannot be there, through no fault of one's own, perhaps one is ill and must stay in bed, and misses a great opportunity. Consequences proceed without regard for my good intentions (although good intentions also have consequences), as if each movement I make makes ripples in the lake. One may know that this is true, but it is very hard to accept. It isn't the acts themselves for which one is responsible—we have so little control over what we do; we are so incontinent; more often than we know it's true that we "couldn't help it"—one is responsible "only" to accept their consequences, to acknowledge that this is a result of how I am.

Responsibility changes very much one's ideas of blame and of guilt. Guilt and blame look backward to the act, as if it could be undone, and are a way of *not* accepting the consequences, of avoiding acceptance. This is not to say that acceptance is unfeeling, quite the contrary. It is only by acceptance that one can experience a depth of gratitude or of regret that is ordinarily quite unknown to us. And these more appropriate feelings, quite unlike guilt, can indeed change us, not only inwardly but also outwardly, in our acts themselves.

I shouted at my student—to help her. Did it? I wanted, by this means, by shouting, to stiffen her for a moment, so that her hands would become steady, so that she would have the sensation of bringing the clay on center, a sensation she could return to later, on her own. It was intended as a "push" to get her over an obstacle she seemed not to be able to pass alone. But it is terribly presumptuous to push anyone, and it is the presumptuousness in myself, the attitude in myself that at that moment assumed the *right* to shout at her, that makes me feel ashamed. The shouting itself is nothing, just a noise, helpful or not, but the attitude of false superiority in me just then was harmful to me and to her. We take in not only words but the attitude of the speaker. We take in with our daily bread the attitude of the baker. No wonder we find it necessary to be armored; another's malice can make me ill, and if I am falsely superior I put in her by stealth the corrosive poison of false inferiority. Another time one can shout, the same thing exactly, and the inner attitude is different, more open, more vulnerable; one can shout with respect, and it is just the right thing, a help for both of us.

The student and the teacher both need help. They exist together in a "teaching situation" so that through the exchange between them help for each participant will be called into being. The teacher easily can take his role in the exchange too seriously, imagining that he himself is called upon to help the student, to decide between types of help, to choose between craftsmanship and interiorization, to choose and to act far beyond his extremely limited powers. He wants to help the student to live better, but is his own life so rich, so fine, so free from error? This task, which he takes on himself through a mistaken sense of responsibility, a task far beyond his power, makes him tense. He becomes enmeshed in local and minor considerations and loses contact with himself. He thinks of help in a pluralistic way, this sort of help, or that sort, and forgets that help is singular, always in the direction of unity, that help is always help-to-Be.

But what shall I *do?* The student is here; I need to talk, move, act; I need to have a plan.

The attitude that help is needed and that it will not come from me directly (although surely my actions and even words can be helpful), an attitude that one could realistically call prayer, releases the tension that otherwise binds and constrains action. I will speak and act anyway, with or without knowledge of my limitations. Isn't it better to know? Perhaps I will plan longer, think more practically, be less enamored of my supposed understanding; perhaps I will be more sane.

Almost all beginners, learning the craft of pottery, make the same errors, have in certain phases of centering the clay, opening it out, and drawing up a cylinder, similar difficulties. They can be told and shown what to do, and they learn. Some of their difficulties are, or seem to be, simply muscular, matters of technique, and others, the more individual difficulties, seem to be rooted in the particular psychology of the student. This has, in any case, been my assumption. But as time passed and I saw so many students, one universal error, for which there seems to be no physical reason, drew my interest and has led me to a new way of questioning both teaching and learning.

The student tries to center the clay. He has difficulty keeping his hands still and the unevenly rotating ball of clay causes his hands to move along its surface, to "ride" the clay instead of controlling it. He braces his elbows on his thighs and manages to bring the clay more into center. But then, then, in taking his hands away from the clay, he does something extra, something unnecessary—he gives the clay a kind of pat, and throws it off center again. Why? There is hardly a beginner who doesn't do this. I can stand or sit next to him and give the most careful directions: "Leave your hands on the clay but relax the pressure. Now just withdraw your hands quietly." But in the last moment, as if saying "There!" the student's hands make that little move that undoes his work. I have even asked the student to press his hand against the flat metal at the side of the wheel and withdraw it, just to show him how to release pressure simply, without that little involuntary comment that the hands seem to make all by themselves. Nobody fails to learn eventually and I have, with each student, remembered again this tiny universal quirk, so small, so easy to discount, that has puzzled my idle curiosity so briefly but so often. Until one day, shaking my head and laughing to myself about it yet again, I said to myself: Well, it's no wonder this happens; none of us knows how to let go of anything—and stopped myself by the thought and began to think if it might be true, if it might be the explanation.

Now, whether this particular explanation is completely or partially true, or whether it isn't, a much more serious question about the implications of education in a craft comes up. Does something learned in one area of the complex human organism cross over into other areas? What is the mechanism? That is, if a person learns to let go of the clay, does that teach him anything at all about "letting go" in other areas of his life? Are the techniques of a craft true educative means—do they educate the whole person—or are they just self-limited and self-contained within the craft? Putting aside for the moment the direct psychological effects of working at a craft—such effects as dealing with impatience or relating to other people or my desire to make something beautiful—putting all those undoubtedly important aspects of crafts work aside, do the technical skills learned in a craft have a hidden penetration into the deeper levels of consciousness that generate attitudes?

On the one hand, I have witnessed many times in myself that thoughts and good intentions are walled off from the body so that I don't act as my reason tells me I should. I acknowledge, even though I don't like it, that I'm a mixture rather than a compound, and that aspects of myself, parts, are, as it were, around the corner and out of sight of other parts.

On the other hand, I believe that the complexity and abundance of forms in the world are governed by an economy of meanings, and that it is these meanings that make one thing analogous to another at a level deeper or wider than either form.

When we speak about education, what are we speaking about? Is it the education of a part only, or is there a real crossing over, a kind of synesthesia not limited to the sense perceptions but affecting feelings and that remarkable amalgam of thought and feeling we refer to as attitudes? Are there modes, means, that can travel freely through us without being halted at the borders of all our separate countries? Can the feelings learn through the body and the thought be informed, not through "interpreting," but by having opened to it new pathways, new ways of thinking?

The world of symbol has been approached by artists of all times. The modern artist attempts to pass into it and return through his feelings, sometimes quite powerfully, but frequently at great cost to himself—he pays the price of losing his balance, overreaching with the emotions at the expense of mind and sometimes of body. Extreme cases of this are easy to find (insanity, alcoholism, ridiculous pride), but just speaking mildly, most of the artists we know are a bit peculiar. The artist attempts to open himself to the passage of forces for which he is not prepared and it can be, if he succeeds, like taking a drug, releasing in himself a great energy that burns with whatever fuel it can find—the coarse material of his undisciplined, ordinary emotions. Many paintings affect us with the force of bad dreams. The modern artist elevates the subjective—he is what precise religious terminology would call an idolater.

So it must be either that painting, to speak of it as an example of art, is not taught as a craft should be, or that the means of a craft, the techniques, are insufficient in themselves to educate, prepare, the whole person.

In ourselves there is an underground stream, a dark reservoir, which we have been calling the symbolic and could as well call symbolic mind. Psychologists, trying to understand, have spoken of an unconscious or subconscious and have attempted to chart certain pathways, usually of the pathological.

Without that dark stream, its action in us, we are dead —cut off from the continuity of life, from participation in intelligence. In it, we are helpless and buffeted about, literally at sea. Damned if we don't, in hell if we do. All of purposeful human life from this point of view, religion, science, art, has been the attempt to build ships.

It may be true that craft was created as a means of educating people in certain attitudes indispensable to a safe voyage on the high sea, but it doesn't seem to be doing its job. Craftsmen don't seem to be any better off than anyone else.

When we ask how, or if, the learning of the techniques

of a craft affects the whole person through the symbology of what he does with his body, there seems to be no answer forthcoming.

We know only direct routes, the strategies of the known, and craft is subtle. As chess is not physical war, but psychic war, the means of discovering a safe passage to the king, past all impediments, diagonal, straightforward, and L-shaped, so the means of a craft, the techniques, are subtle strategies, indirect routes. And if the strategy of the means is subtle, how much more so must the goal be.

Just as chess, for all its fascination, can be played without reference to or understanding of what the game of chess symbolizes, so craft can be no more than known means to a known end.

It falls upon the teacher to be a strategist of subtle means, to confound the student, to arrest his more facile understanding, to prevent him from resting content with his assumptions, to thwart him, bedevil him, confuse him, all in the guise of helpfulness. It falls upon the teacher to arouse in the student the emotional need to approach the craft differently by blocking in him any satisfaction that can be found in his customary means of approach. And this the teacher must do not from a comfortable distance but with immediacy, in the thick of battle, in the heat of his own unknown, his own fears, his own confusion.

A student, treated this way, is bound to become confused and depressed and to complain, to himself at least, that everything he does seems to be wrong. It isn't possible to learn when someone is, however subtly, always saying "No" to you, unless the "No" is grounded in a bigger "Yes." The student is continually being discouraged by the teacher and that would be fine, just as long as he is being encouraged at the same time, encouraged, that is, not by the progress he's making but by sometimes coming in contact with a better system of values than the one he sees himself clinging to so tenaciously. This "Yes," this possibility which he can be forgiven for imagining that his teacher has already attained to, can give him hope and help him to bear his increasing recognition of how little he understands. The teacher, laboring on the same path, but with greater certainty that the search he is engaged in is not illusory, needs to search for an understanding that is not at the mercy of dualism.

An exceptionally talented student brought the issue to me from another direction. In this case, the student very quickly and with hardly any effort began to turn out quite commendable pottery. The pots were unimaginative but strong and vigorous in form, light and well thrown. He was happy and I was at a loss. I found myself looking at his work to find fault with it, to try to slow him down, to shake his self-confidence, to find an opening in him that would allow a question to come in, a search to appear. This particular student left, studied silk screening for a while, then went on to photography before I lost touch with him. He skimmed the surface of everything. I sometimes think it was a pity, that if only I had been more rigorous with him all that talent could have called forth something deeper in him than it did. And I wonder how to think about the differences between people. Do some people, however gifted, simply lack the wish to find a real home in themselves? Are there some whom ill-fortune has doomed never to become interested even in the possibility?

If the senses are dense, distracted, one will not hear even one's own name being called. The technical aspects of a craft cannot have their full impact on the deeper receptors of the symbolic mind when the feelings are dull or occupied with other matters. Something has to call the feelings to the matter at hand, to engage them in the craft. Pridefulness, the fear of failing, the ambition to succeed, the emotions aroused by the struggle with difficulties, found in abundance in all of us, help to call the attention. But, while they open a channel to more interior regions of receptivity, they also fill it with their own considerable noise. Something from the interior needs to come to answer then, to quiet the noise.

At first the student is stirred up, agitated by the frustration of not being able to do with his hands what he wishes with his mind to do. Something, not only the body, doesn't obey him. It gets in the way. The teacher tries to "help" but, although what the teacher says and shows seems quite clear, the difficulties only increase. The student is angry with himself, tries harder, fails again. And again. In the corner of his "eye" he catches a flicker of something, like a thought but unlike it. He tries to look at it directly but it evades him, vanishes. He starts to work more carefully, alertly, hoping to catch sight of it again. Without realizing it he becomes less agitated. Instead of pushing at the craft he is being drawn by it, called by an echo in himself.

It must have been just such a process that led the young woman I spoke of earlier to her new understanding of the need for "sensitivity and firmness." It requires a struggle for an opening to appear and it requires quiet for it not to close again at once.

Now, to ask again, because the question still nags at me: Granted that the technical means of a craft, through struggle with the not-only-physical difficulties that they present to the student, and through the assistance of a teacher, can on occasion open a channel to the symbolic world, is the student's access to that channel limited to his experiences in the studio, or can it encompass more of his life? Does anybody really *change* by studying a craft? Isn't that the question? Because if there is no actual change, if all we are left with are a few pleasant pots and some interesting ideas, a handful of experiences, is that enough? It can be a great deal, perhaps more than we deserve, but is it enough to satisfy us?

To backtrack for a moment: We don't know which change is trivial and which is important. The characteristics we see in ourselves and most despise may be no more than surface manifestations and not worth concerning ourselves about. The changes we hope for, dream about, may be childish or impossible. We are captured by our belief in the manifest, even here, in our most felt hopes, and long to *act* differently, to *feel* differently, not really to *be different*.

Every cause has its effect. Everything I live through has an effect on me; every experience, every taste, every impression, is like a tiny push that affects the direction of my life. Most pushes have little force and the cumulative effect of all the already established opinions and habits and other modes of my life present a counterthrust that keeps me, usually, more or less as I am.

Actual change, unmistakable change, begins with change of attitude. Attitude is like a magnet—it attracts like experiences, reinforces itself. The inner affects the outer much more than the other way around, at least in adults.

And each one of us has made, early in his life, a "bad bargain," has given up a large chunk of his openness, different for different people, in order to get by with a minimum of pain. This "bad bargain" forms, or, to put it more strongly, *is* our predominant attitude.

How can a craft insinuate its way past an unconsciously constructed barricade and plant in the deepest part a new growth that can find its way to the light? (In one version of the story, the prince didn't just kiss Sleeping Beauty; he impregnated her.)

The craft does not appear to threaten anything established in us. It is, especially for those of us living today, something external to our lives, an addendum, a pleasure rather than a necessity. The laws of the craft, the order of the "moves," are fixed with no reference to the student— he cannot take them personally. He learns them, practices them, repeats them. It becomes true for him that the inside shape of the pot determines the outside—it is simply so, physically, not philosophically. He learns that he has to wait to pull up the walls of the pot until the inside base is prepared, flat and as wide as the completed pot will need. He learns to keep the uppermost edge of the cylinder compressed because he will need it to be in good condition later on when he comes to finish the lip of the pot. He may learn that Form comes from something like "grace," although grace is not what he imagined it was, and requires mind.

Perhaps none of this will affect him deeply. It depends on how willing he is to confront the fact that the way he has been accustomed to work falls short of responding to the call of the craft. It depends on his determination, his sincerity, on how much he values the strange taste of something new that now and then comes his way. It depends somewhat on who his teacher is. It depends on the type and the extent of the "bad bargain" that structures his inner psyche. It depends very much on what he wants, even though, at the beginning, he might not know that he wants something.

I see that in putting the question, again and again, over these last few pages, I have expected a substantive answer —yes or no. But the craft can have a transforming effect upon us only if we bring ourselves to the craft. The secret of how to work, which is the secret of how to live, begins with the need to learn.

ABOUT THE AUTHOR

Carla Needleman was an occasional potter
for twenty years and currently is completing a book
that demystifies medicine. She was born in New York City,
is the mother of two children, Raphael and Eve,
and lives in San Francisco.